T0062773

"Having experienced three of the four types of dreams which come to humans as they sleep, in search of answers to my questions I perused many of the 'dream' books with their cookie cutter interpretations. I ended up with even more questions. What a precious gift this author has given us: A way to look to our inner self for the answers we seek. A way to make sense of our dreams and perhaps wake with a clear picture of the path we are meant to take. By sharing her journey with us, we know we are not alone, and by the end of the journey I hope she can tell us if butterflies do dream."

—MARY ANN GOVE,
AUTHOR, COLUMNIST, AND POET FEATURED IN WOMAN'S DAY, ARIZONA HIGHWAYS, WOMAN'S WORLD AND MANY OF THE READER'S DIGEST REIMAN PUBLICATIONS

"A practical guide to becoming more aware of the keys to your past, present and future so that you can embody more of your divine self in your everyday life."

—NANCY CONNOR,
FOUNDER AND CHAIR OF RINGING ROCKS FOUNDATION

"It was so refreshing to read Laina's chapters on dreams. She seems to have much experience in this area with terrific insights. This is something everyone could benefit from. I am anxiously awaiting more from Laina on this subject of dream interpretation."

—MERRILL DASTRUP

"*Do Butterflies Dream* is a divinely guided instruction book on how to analyze ones dreams. Laina provides enlightening examples that take the reader step by step through the process. This is the first dream analysis book that I truly understand and can follow easily. What a wonderful tool to assist in one's life journey!"

—CHRISTINA LUFKIN,
AUTHOR OF *LIVE WITH PURPOSE: DIE WITH DIGNITY*, *THE RIPPLE EFFECT: STORIES FROM THE HEART* BY CHRISTINA LUFKIN AND FRIENDS.
WWW.CHRISTINALUFKIN.WEEBLY.COM

"Laina Lloyd's *Do Butterflies Dream?* provides wonderful insights into interpreting dreams. It helps the reader understand what his or her subconscious mind is expressing and is invaluable for all those on a quest of self improvement."

—SY BRANDON,
AUTHOR OF "LIFE IS A HAMMOCK"

"*Do Butterflies Dream* by Laina Lloyd is an inspired and insightful guidebook to help one discover the hidden meaning of their dreams. The many interesting dream examples and possible interpretations that are shared effectively help illustrate the process."

—ANITA LUCIA RANUCCI

Do
Butterflies
Dream?

LAINA LLOYD

abbott press

Copyright © 2014 Laina Lloyd.

All rights reserved. No part of this book may be used or reproduced by
any means, graphic, electronic, or mechanical, including photocopying,
recording, taping or by any information storage retrieval system
without the written permission of the publisher except in the case
of brief quotations embodied in critical articles and reviews.

Abbott Press books may be ordered through
booksellers or by contacting:

Abbott Press
1663 Liberty Drive
Bloomington, IN 47403
www.abbottpress.com
Phone: 1-866-697-5310

Cover photo—Shawn and Sadie Connolly
Front Cover Model—Shalane Moore-Williams
Inside cover photo—Shalane Moore-Williams
Inside cover model—Charlotte

Because of the dynamic nature of the Internet, any web
addresses or links contained in this book may have changed
since publication and may no longer be valid. The views
expressed in this work are solely those of the author and do
not necessarily reflect the views of the publisher, and the
publisher hereby disclaims any responsibility for them.

Any people depicted in stock imagery provided by Thinkstock are
models, and such images are being used for illustrative purposes only.
Certain stock imagery © Thinkstock.

ISBN: 978-1-4582-1719-6 (sc)
ISBN: 978-1-4582-1720-2 (e)

Library of Congress Control Number: 2014912843

Printed in the United States of America.

Abbott Press rev. date: 08/06/2014

This book is dedicated to my mother,
my dream counselor,
my mentor,
my hero,
my friend.

Contents

Forward

We all have dreams, but why do we have them? What if anything can be gained by understanding them? Are there universal interpretation methods that are accurate? Can the necessary information be obtained through self-dream interpretation, or is professional consultation needed?

Dreams provide an easy unique way to communicate with an immense veiled capacity of the mind. This part of the mind is crying out through repetition, or images which may seem bizarre or nonsensical to the conscious mind, often warning or giving excellent counsel for a particular problem or situation. Pay attention! Stop ignoring or misinterpreting this extremely wise personal counselor.

In today's world, information is abundant and books are an amazingly inexpensive way to get valuable information, but what information is really worth taking the time to read and understand? When someone spends thousands of hours focusing on one subject, their understanding and application of that subject is worth close consideration. This is the case with Laina Lloyd and the subject of understanding dreams. Through many years of daily dream interpretation she constantly hones her knowledge and skills. She has chosen to share her in-depth knowledge about a life changing subject through this amazing book.

Do Butterflies Dream? clearly teaches correct dream interpretation principals. Each key concept is simply illustrated through straightforward expression and numerous interesting dream examples. Through reading other's dreams, and seeing the positive results that come through accurate understanding, we gain the courage to trust our own best counselor. Please enjoy this down-to-earth book and use the practical techniques, enriching your life more and more each time you use them.

—ALLEN J. SMITHSON
Author of *The Parable of the Hand and the Glove, A Spiritual Awakening*

Preface

Butterflies

"It is eternity now. I am in the midst of it.
It is about me in the sunshine;
I am in it, as the butterfly in the light-laden air.
Nothing has come; it is now.
Now is eternity; now is the immortal life."
—Richard Jefferies
The Story of My Heart (1883)

One morning while sitting in my back yard, enjoying the warm sunshine, multicolored wild flowers and the peace that a quiet moment can bring, I noticed a stunningly beautiful butterfly. Amazement and curiosity overcame me and I longed to know about this enchanting little creature. In Scottsdale, Arizona, there is a magical place called Butterfly Wonderland. This spot is the home of America's largest butterfly atrium. I knew I had to visit this "wonderland" and acquire more knowledge about one of God's most glorious creations;

the butterfly, a symbol of rebirth and transformation into brilliance!

Upon entering the atrium filled with these charming, fairy like beings, I felt an overwhelming urge to cry. Butterflies of all colors, shapes and sizes silently wafted over head, circling around me with grace and beauty. All I could do was stand there in utter amazement in their presence. It was as if I was transported to another world, a type of dream world, a place filled with fairies, elves, enchantment and fantasy where all your desires and wishes come true. Ethereal music could be heard over hidden speakers, soft gentle mists of warm water stirred my senses, and winding brick pathways invited me to enter this sacred wonderland. Walking with reverence for the safety of these fragile beings, I proceeded, eyes wide, giggling with a childlike innocence.

It was during this type of hypnotic state of joy that I wondered, "Do butterflies dream?" Scientific research has revealed that all mammals dream. Dogs have been observed barking and running while sleeping. Cats scratch in the air at imaginary critters, and from experiments researchers have learned that even finches replay their daily melodies in dreams. Recent studies have revealed that more animals dream than has previously been believed. Sleep patterns which influence dreaming are not the same for all species. For example, dolphins do a type of slow circle swimming where it appears that only half their brain is sleeping at one time.

Smaller animals have more REM sleep than larger ones. Elephants only need three to five hours of sleep in a twenty-four hour period, while the ground squirrel may need up to twenty hours of sleep in a day. New discoveries about dreaming are regularly occurring, but so far it is not yet known how or why animals dream. Researchers also do not know if insects, or more specifically butterflies, dream. While it is uncertain whether butterflies dream, it is apparent that people do. Dreams and their meanings have been the subject of human thought since the beginning of time.

Within these pages there is a wonderland of dreams filled with key symbols and messages to help with understanding the hidden meanings experienced in the magical world of dreams. Whether the dream is about flying high above the trees, entertaining a mysterious lover, or has a prophetic message, this book is designed to be a guide in helping to understand the hidden symbols and communications being received. By analyzing dreams, there is an increase in awareness within the conscious realm where the dreamer can receive assistance with their personal transformation into expanding brilliance!

Introduction

> "We are so captivated by and entangled in our
> subjective consciousness that we have forgotten
> the age-old fact that God speaks chiefly
> through dreams and visions."
> —Carl Jung

At some time or another, everyone has had thought experiences which could be called dreaming. They may take the form of a nocturnal dream, a daydream, an impression, vision, consistent enjoyment of a certain type of story, or even the unpleasant recurrence of life dilemmas. Having an understanding of the interpretation of these situations may reveal the keys, not only to a near conscious state of being, but also to dreams. Every dream, no matter how strange it may seem, has something to tell. There is a magical wonderland of memories, instincts, emotions and understandings located within the soul.

Many dream symbols are universal; however, dreamer's symbols will have unique personal meaning.

Dreams cannot use the conscious mind language to tell their story. It is necessary for them to speak in parables and allegories; so symbols are used to picture their meanings. These symbols are considered to be the language of the soul. Ultimately the only accurate interpretation of a dream experience is made from the dreamer's feelings and experiences with the dream symbols.

There are basically four ways in which most people experiences dreams. Some dreams are influenced by a physical stimulus which can impress specific ideas on the corporeal brain. For example, when I am in a deep sleep I periodically dream of being chased by a roaring lion or angry bear. I wake up startled only to realize that what appeared to be a wild animal in my dream was in reality, my external senses trying to make meaning of my husband snoring! Because of this, it is important to take note of the physical and mental surroundings of the dreamer when interpreting dreams.

All life experiences are stored in the subconscious mind. For the purpose of this book the subconscious is the part of the mind which is not fully aware but which influences actions and feelings. These memories are occasionally filtered through the mind into a conscious awareness by way of dreams. There are dreams that are influenced by subconscious memory. Events of the day are often re-lived. Bothersome situations or ideas may manifest in a dream, or items of deep concern can trigger an emblematic dream. In instances like these, the subconscious often enlightens the dreamer with symbolic information that may help them in their waking moments.

The telepathic dream forms a connection between

dreamers where one is the sender and the other is the receiver. This can happen in sleep with minds that have a strong affinity with each other such as a man and wife, a mother and her child or close business associates.

The astral dream experience happens when the ego, or consciousness, experiences a dream similar to an out of body projection, an occurrence where the spirit travels outside of the body. These dreams involve visiting distant places, visions, communicating with the dead, or the receiving of premonitions—a prophetic type dream.

When I was a small child my mother told me the Bible story about Joseph, a young man who often had prophetic dreams. He was sold into Egypt because of the jealousy of his brothers. In the Old Testament, Genesis chapter thirty seven, we learn that Joseph was loved by his father Jacob more than all his children because he was the youngest son of his old age. Joseph's father made him a coat of many colors. When Joseph's brothers saw that their father loved him more than all of them, they chose to hate and despise him.

One night, Joseph dreamed a dream and he shared it with his brothers. In the dream Joseph was told that he would one day rule over his brothers. Sharing this information with them created even stronger feelings of jealousy, so they planned a way to get rid of him. Eventually Joseph was sold into Egypt by his brothers, where he remained for many years.

Through a course of events that happened in his life, Joseph wrongfully ended up in prison. In prison he became known as one who could interpret dreams. One day the Pharaoh called for Joseph to help him interpret a disturbing dream. He told Joseph that he could not find anyone who could interpret his dream. Joseph told Pharaoh that by the spirit of God he could interpret his dream and give him peace. As a result of the interpretation of his dream, and the peace he received from it, Pharaoh entrusted Joseph to be a great ruler in his kingdom, second in command to the Pharaoh himself. This responsibility given to Joseph proved to be a blessing to many people in Pharaoh's kingdom, including Joseph's own family.

Because of this story and how it impressed me as a little child, along with my mother's teachings about dream interpretation and skill as a dream counselor, I often found myself asking for the gift to interpret dreams. When faced with challenging situations in my life or when in need of answers to personal questions, I would ask for guidance in a dream to assist me on my path. Through the gifts of the spirit, or what is occasionally referred to as the universal life force, and my desire to know the meanings of dreams, I have received valuable guidance. This knowledge has helped me to assist not only myself and family, but others as well.

As I continued to gain a reputation for accurate dream interpretation, and effective dream counseling, more and more people began to tell or send me their dreams. This book contains excerpts from the many hundreds of dreams that have been shared. I expect that by reading the pages in this book, you too will learn about the meanings in your dreams and be guided on your life journey. All dreams have purpose. Can you be certain that your dreams are less important than Joseph's? My desire is that by reading this book you will receive the gift of interpretation which may be the key that can unlock the purpose of your life through the marvels of your mind.

Chapter 1

Sleep Opens the Door

"All that is comes from the mind; it is based on the mind,
it is fashioned by the mind."
—The Pali Cannon 500-250 BC

*A*n unusual dream came to me one night. I found myself in a casino needing to use the bathroom. The friend I was with, who was a female, said "Laina, you get paid money here for how much you eliminate." "What? Seriously?" I asked. I then proceeded to fill the toilet, imagining my release as quarters. After flushing the toilet, I went to the cashier's cage and was promptly handed three $20 dollar bills and one $10 dollar bill for a total of $70.00! I was so excited that I ran to my friend showing her how much I received! When I awoke, I thought, "Now that was a strange dream!"

Embarrassing as it is to share this dream, a quick analysis will help discover the hidden dream meaning. The dream's starting place was a casino, which according to the dictionary is a public room or building where gambling games are played. If assisting in the dream interpretation of another person, you would ask them what a casino means by saying, "Assume that I am unfamiliar with the term 'casino.' In your own words, explain what a casino means or represents to you." Since the dream is mine, I acknowledge that a casino is a place of gambling and feel that I am in a place which is risky. In this place I relieve myself. To me this represents eliminating something deep inside, something extremely personal and perhaps embarrassing, by letting it pass through and out of me. Not only do I eliminate, but I receive payment for it! I love getting money and enjoy what money can do in my life. Receiving money for elimination is exciting and creates a desire to eliminate more.

I also find myself with a female friend. Generally, when a person has a dream about a female, the female most often represents a specific feeling or emotion. This female was a friend, someone that I was close to, but not related to. Symbolically she represents a friendly feeling and emotion that is close to me, but not related to me.

At this point, I should share more information to assist with the understanding about what this dream message is for me. A few weeks before my dream, I was seriously considering writing a book about dreams. Dreams may provide ways to wellness and healing by expanding awareness, allowing internal emotional release. I began feeling that a book would be a great way to assist others on their wellness journey. I thought, "I wish I could come up with a title or format for my book. Knowing this may help me focus and accelerate my book creation."

After stating my wish, feelings of inadequacy and concern began to surface. I frequently heard a voice within saying, "Who are you to write a book? You don't know anything, and books are very personal, especially a book about dreams!" Then the dream came. Because of my dream, I received the realization that writing a book is a gamble. It may prove to be embarrassing because I will be sharing some of my innermost feelings and beliefs (the elimination). However, I may also receive financial rewards for this elimination, which would be very exciting! At the time of the dream, the thought of writing a book was just a casual feeling and emotion, (represented by my friend) that was friendly and supportive to me.

There it is, an unusual dream with a profound personal meaning. Why was it so unusual? It seemed unusual, even humorous, because dreams speak in symbols and/or allegories which may at first appear abstract and unrelated. After understanding the meaning of the symbols, or what can be called the "soul language," these dreams make total sense. Most dreamers have made the familiar comment, "Now that was a strange dream!" The dream may seem strange until the symbolic language of emotions is untangled revealing a logical message.

The mind contains knowledge and information which seemingly has been forgotten and can be recalled with some conscious effort. Subtle whispers of buried memories come floating into consciousness at the oddest times and places. Karol Truman, author of the book *Feelings Buried Alive Never Die*, teaches that negative feelings are not always resolved, and they can remain alive in the psyche, or body energy field. Sometimes these unresolved feelings can affect lives and actions. Candice Pert, Ph.D., author of *Molecules of Emotion,* believes that the body is the unconscious mind; that overwhelming emotions create trauma and those emotions are stored in different parts of the body. For the purpose of this book the unconscious is the part of the mind that is inaccessible to the conscious mind which affects behavior and emotions. The unconscious consists of the cognitive processes that occur automatically. Behaviors and emotions, whether negative or positive, are very real and can manifest in dreams revealing a need to be dealt with and released.

Dreams can be understood and this understanding can be learned. To realize the meaning of dreams, ask for guidance from the unseen aspect of life that seems to be connected to everyone and everything (Carl Jung calls it God, I call it spirit). Through spirit, learning can take place to assist with interpreting what dreams are telling. Discovering what dreams are conveying is like turning a key that will unlock buried treasures or even false beliefs held over from childhood.

There are some who say, "I never dream." There may be several reasons for this. One reason may be a satisfied interest in their daily living, finding it so satisfying that there is no curiosity whatsoever in any vague or obscure inner dream process. Others may be the type who ignore dreams because they are in a comfortable emotional resting place and desire to stay there for their lifetime. According to Edgar Cayce, the most documented psychic of the twentieth century, there are four reasons someone would forget their dreams. They may have a lack of interest, may be experiencing physical exhaustion, have impurities in the body, or be strongly connected to a life of materialistic concerns.

Dreams are sometimes forgotten because they are dealing with emotional problems that may be too frightening for the individual to face, while others awaken quite suddenly and are unable to catch even a passing glimpse of scenes which they have been viewing in their sleep.

While experiencing feelings that it is important to recall night dreams, ask spirit for help to remember and find answers through dreaming. It is possible to recollect dreams and develop the ability to recall details. Always keep a notebook or recording device by the side of the bed to assist the subconscious mind in connecting with the conscious mind. These devices act as tools to help remember the choice to recall and record dreams. If no dreams manifest or can be remembered, this book can still open a new awareness. Many of the principles it outlines can be applied to life's circumstances which seem to recur, as well as situations which leave strong emotional memories. When lessons that life's conditions are trying to teach go unheeded, chances are there will be more similar circumstances to look forward to!

The interpretation of dreams will come with study and practice. Dreams are speaking from an obscure area of consciousness. Henri Bergson, author of *Dreams,* believes that, "The role of the brain is to bring back the remembrance of an action, to prolong the remembrance in movements." The subconscious mind is full of vision and insight, with a large amount of memory. Bergson believes that we live in a world of perceptions, "Which reappear in sleep," and that the sense of perception is, "Far from being narrowed during sleep at all points, is on the contrary extended, at least in certain directions, in its field of operations."

Yacki Raizizun, Ph. D. and author of *The Secret of Dreams,* believes that in sleep, the dreamer frequently goes over his life in a type of "phantom fashion," living over the experiences of the day. "Very often the ego enlightens the sleeper of some material thing for his own benefit, which he may use advantageously in his waking state, but as he generally looks at the phenomena of dreams as a hallucination of the brain, he allows many a golden opportunity to slip through his fingers because the materialist's brain cannot grasp things of the spirit."

While it is often quite simple to see the dream meaning emerging from behind the perceptions of someone else, each person has their own memories and insights and cannot always see what lies behind them. After becoming aware that dreams do have meaning, the dreamer will begin to get glimpses from their own dreams which will be advantageous as they begin to help other dreamers. Go slowly with the desire to give advice while interpreting other people's dreams. Support an attitude of love and understanding, and remember that the field of dreams is sacred ground. The unselfish person can be of much service to others, but this requires knowledge and humility.

Chapter 2

The Fantastic Journey

"Dreams are the preview of your potential possibilities."
—*anonymous*

*D*reams affect emotional tone and life reactions whether or not the dreamer has any awareness of the dreams or reactions to them. Dreams have always constituted a sort of "play-therapy" room if nothing else. They are a place to go where negative emotions can dissipate. The dream is a safe place to slug someone who has created an internal personal conflict, or perhaps, it is a place where pushing a dominating person over a cliff is possible. The dreamer can even wake up feeling less guilty, because they are relieved to find that they didn't really do such terrible things.

Nightmares sometimes lessen the sense of guilt or frustration by allowing the process of acting out punishments and tortures. The dreamer awakens feeling that they have in some way atoned or released their anger and pain. Dreams justifying dependencies may occur in which terrible things happen because the dreamer is not being taken care of by others. This makes the dreamer feel justified in demanding protection, validating their refusal to become secure and independent. They may maintain their inaction and apathy by picturing in dreams the catastrophes that could overtake them if they were forced to take action.

Dreaming of success may ease the pain of failures, thus seeing things turn out better than expected. Making peace with a present situation is done through dreams by dramatizing one's self into worse predicaments, then awakening relieved to discover that it was only a dream. Brave stands are taken in dreams where there may be a lack of courage in conscious moments. By taking a bold position in dreams, there can be enough relief to ease the pain of failures in conscious time, which may enable endurance for real life situations. This type of dream process may help stall a scolding to the person who is overly imposing, before the maturity to handle the consequences of such a drastic move is consciously available.

Dreams of forewarning sometimes create a desire to delay impulsive actions and cause a more cautious attitude all the next day. The subconscious mind is dedicated to our survival and successfulness, and is using dreams as a guide by bringing to awareness the stored images and memories of a lifetime, perhaps even the memories held within our DNA. The dream teaches and brings comfort to the best of its ability whether the dreamer knows it or the dream is even remembered or not. The feeling with which the dream leaves is sometimes the greatest help even though the dream may be forgotten.

A young client shared a profound dream given to him which was a comfort and guide during a time of turmoil and trials. He said that his dream was a "sweet gift of light and brightness." The dream began with him sitting in a large auditorium while attending a work meeting. Immediately into the dream, and with great horror, he noticed that arms and legs started falling off people who were sitting near him! Then he noticed others in the room who were, "Exploding their guts out all over the place!" and he knew that there was some unseen force trying to destroy everyone. He searched for a safe place to hide and he located a small inconspicuous cooler which would provide cover until the gruesome slaughter was over.

Running toward the cooler, he saw a beautiful blond haired girl, frightened, standing by herself. He encouraged her to get inside the cooler with him until it was safe to come back out. She refused him, so he quickly crawled inside the cooler alone. "I was in the cooler for a long time. After all the mess of blood and carnage was cleared, someone knocked on the cooler door and retrieved me. I noticed the girl, she had miraculously survived! I wanted to give her a flower as a gift of comfort. I found a white flower, bright and full of light, which smelled like vanilla. The scent was sweet and I could sense every internal odor which combined to make the vanilla scent. The flower fragrance was pretty, which felt good. It was a gift."

After the young man gave the beautiful girl his gift, he proceeded to go to a local grocery store to meet his sister who was a clerk employed there. She was to give him a ride home. The sister knew that he had just gone through an extremely traumatic experience, so when they arrived at her place, she took him into the kitchen where she began to nurture him with snacks while he talked about his experience. The dreamer said that they were, "In an atmosphere of comfort where I felt safe to talk about the trauma I had just witnessed."

As we discussed the dream, he shared his current difficulties with finding enjoyable and sustainable employment. The past few years had been extremely stressful for him and his family. One night, he couldn't sleep, so he decided to access the internet and do research about on-line colleges. The more he learned, the better he felt about going to school to continue his education. His decision filled him with a good feeling, like receiving a "sweet gift of light and brightness." A few nights after doing research, he had his dream. He said, "Even though I had been going through a traumatic employment experience, I began to feel that things would eventually work out. Pursuing my college education felt like a comfortable and correct path."

The message this young man received from the dream, even though it started out in a gruesome and horrible manner, left him feeling encouraged about his future. He took a few weeks to research different on-line colleges and found one that he decided would be a good fit for his continuing education. He has completed several courses and is currently in the top of his class.

In dreams we may picture symbols and plots which can give insight into personal shortcomings, show objective views for current life situations, and sometimes bring enjoyable messages that leave impressions of well-being. These messages can help to lessen anxieties, release fear, assist with clarity, and give strength which in turn may help solve daily problems.

Not long ago I developed an abscess on the bottom left side of my jaw. Getting an abscess was surprising because I had just finished receiving extensive work on my teeth costing thousands of dollars. I didn't want to spend more money fixing a tooth that should have already been taken care of! At the dentist visit I was told a root canal had gone bad. In considering the cost of getting this tooth fixed, and my current dental bill at the time, I decided to take a few days to make a decision. In the meantime, I supported my immune system with high doses of vitamin C, therapeutic grade essential oils, natural supplements, a raw food diet, and a form of energy work called Reiki. It was during this time of physical healing and contemplation that a dream manifested as a guide for my dilemma.

The dream began in a large city where trains were driving off the tracks, down the roads, and alongside other vehicles. I was concerned about safety, but noticed that the train engineers were very competent, even better drivers than the car and truck drivers who were all around them. I decided to sit in front of the train, outside on the grill to enjoy a thrilling and invigorating ride! Not long after positioning myself outside the train, I noticed that it began to move toward a wild and overgrown jungle. Feeling concern for my safety, I climbed inside to sit with the other passengers. The men and women on the train thought I was crazy and fearless!

In the next dream scene I was standing in the road on

dry ground. I observed alligators nearby coming out of wet earth, hundreds of them, all crawling in the same direction. There was a man with them. One alligator grabbed his arm, but he pulled away unhurt. I watched this amazingly strong and fearless man enter a cave located in a nearby mountainside. Almost immediately after entering the cave, he exited, running with an enormous herd of wild horned dinosaurs. I was concerned for his safety, but again he remained unhurt. In my amazement, I shouted, "Oh, this man is responsible for the animals!" I noticed them charge forward, courageously, with a specific goal in mind! As I was watching this electrifying scene, I heard the words "Critical mass Laina! Go with it!"

Upon awakening, I asked for guidance to understand the dream's meaning, and was told that the dream message was about healing the abscess with a type of critical mass effort. I needed to go back to the natural, which in the dream was represented by the jungle, animals and nature. Do the natural thing and hit it hard, like a freight train, like the dinosaurs and alligators. Keep the action going until the abscess is healed. I proceeded to do just that and within a week the abscess was gone, and my tooth was saved. Dreams have many functions and this dream was a personal message of action that my subconscious was revealing through one fantastic journey!

A vivid dream was told to me by a young pregnant mother whose husband had recently quit his job. "We were moving to a bigger house and I was thirty-two weeks pregnant. My husband, father, brothers and myself, were in the shed cleaning. We had a lot of furniture and boxes stored in the shed. They moved the washer and dryer out from under a big shelf and set it by the door. I opened the washer to see if we had stored anything inside of it, and a big black widow spider crawled out onto my hand and bit me. After a couple of minutes tending to the bite, I started to feel very dizzy, so my husband rushed me to the hospital. My doctor informed me that if they didn't take the baby out right then via C-section, that the toxins in the spider venom would reach the baby's sac where she would start to drink and the venom would kill her. I asked about an anti-venom shot and they said it was too strong for her little body and it would likely paralyze her for her whole life. I was freaking out and having a nervous breakdown, but of course started screaming, 'Well, get her out then!' I was so worried about her survival at such a young gestation, that I was inconsolable."

After the dream, the young mother had to get up and sit for a while to calm down. She felt relieved that it was only a dream, but the dream had revealed deep emotions of pain, fear, worry and concern for her ability to provide for the new life growing inside her. The timing of the dream was important because it occurred after her husband quit his job. She realized that she was anxious and concerned for their survival with no employment income to help supply their needs as she was preparing to move into a new structure of beliefs (represented by her new home in the dream). New structures of belief often occur when we experience life changes such as the birth of a child, change in employment, a death, marriage, or other strong emotional events.

The anger and frustration this young mother was feeling toward her husband continued revealing itself in dreams where she would often waken feeling betrayed and neglected. She also manifested dreams where she wanted to scratch her husband's eyes out! Dreaming of such things was a natural presentation to the feelings she was experiencing during her waking moments, feelings she could not reveal or express without repercussions. To find relief from some of these strong emotions and concerns that were revealed in her dreams, the young mother became creative in making homemade items for her new child. She started reading uplifting and encouraging quotations and phrases, as well as reaching out to trusted family members and friends for advice and support. Getting a part-time job also helped alleviate some of her financial concerns.

Keeping busy doing constructive activities assisted her with the frustrations she was feeling toward her husband. Her angry dreams began to fade and even though her husband continued in his struggle to find gainful employment, she used her energy in a more positive and uplifting process. Her creative and financially supportive activities provided her with the emotional assistance she required. The young mother gave birth to a beautiful healthy baby girl.

These dreams of violence, flowers, trains, jungles, dinosaurs, and spiders are examples of how problems and strong emotions were revealed to the dreamers. Each message was given in efforts to lessen anxiety, release fear, and bring clarity. Our bodies are made up of cells that are perfect in their expressions. Scientific research suggests that the human brain has a greater number of possible connections among neuron-pathways than there are atomic particles in the universe. We are created from cosmic energy and information, which is available to us through our thoughts. Our soul language will manifest ways for us to fulfill our full potential and one of those ways is through fantastic journeys brought to us through the window of our dreams.

Chapter 3

Here We Go Again

*"Your vision will become clear only when you
look into your heart....Who looks outside, dreams.
Who looks inside, awakens.*
—Carl Jung

Recurring Dreams and Life Situations

My mother always listened to my dreams and because of her training as a dream counselor, she understood what I was feeling and thinking. For example, in one of my repeating dreams I would often find myself sitting precariously high on a tall white pedestal, scared, feeling helpless and on my own. I saw no way to get back to the ground. With tears streaming down my face I sat afraid and immovable on my pedestal of fear. After experiencing my dream and upon awakening I would usually be crying. My mother would come to my bedside and ask about my dream.

Later in life when I was older and more mature, mom told me that as I related this dream to her she would realize I was experiencing feelings of unworthiness. I felt that she had put me on a pedestal of what she called, "Overwhelming expectations." Although it was my dream, she saw a message revealed in the dream about herself, a message to back off on her desires and actions projected toward me. This allowed me to feel safe with less pressure to perform which brought relief from what I sensed were her, "Overwhelming expectations."

A young single mother shared a recurring dream where she would find herself walking through a familiar house, lost and wandering. In the most recent of these recurring dreams, and for the first time, she saw herself walking through the front door. On this door she began to notice several written messages she hadn't seen until this dream. The messages were tattered, old and weathered and had been there all along.

The young mother mentioned that she recently changed her life path by choosing to listen to subtle messages that she felt were guiding her. She affirmed that her actions of listening to and accepting guidance, were the reason her recurring house dream changed. Messages were represented in the dream by notes on the door that had been there, unseen, all along. Because she changed her life path and started listening to her subtle messages, the original recurring dream of wandering and feeling lost stopped manifesting.

Some dreams recur and have different endings, depending on the dreamer's maturity and belief state at the time. In a particular dream, a young teenage dreamer goes to garage sales with his father and mother. In one version of the dream they are parked on a steep hill, but on the way back, the hill seems to get steeper. The boy and his family barely make it across the road, where they find some trees to grasp as they steady themselves while they descend the steep hill. They are doing their best to get back down the hill to their vehicle. The boy's mother, being overweight, loses her step and begins to fall. The boy's father goes after her trying to save her. The boy clings onto the trees, but loses his step and falls.

In another version of the young man's recurring dream, he goes with his father and mother to yard sales. They are parked on a steep hill. On the way back, the hill seems to get steeper. The boy and his family barely make it across the road, where they find some trees to grasp as they steady themselves while they make their descent. They are doing their best to get back down the hill to their vehicle. The boy's mother, being overweight, loses her step and begins to fall. The boy's father goes after her trying to save her. Again, as with the first dream, the mother and father eventually fall down the steep hill, but this time the boy enjoys the climb, never falls, and does not miss his parents one bit!

When people dream of family relations, especially mothers and fathers, the relatives are often symbols of closely related actions and ideas (the father), and closely related feelings and emotions (the mother). As a teen, the boy and his family would often go to yard sales together, which symbolized an activity that represented family closeness. Current life experiences the boy had been going through, such as challenges at home and situations with his parents, changed. This change affected his beliefs about his family. This new perspective in the boy's belief system created a different outcome in his recurring dream.

A friend of mine often experiences recurring dreams that she feels have a positive influence on how she views her family, especially her husband. One particular dream she had was with vivid colors. She and her husband bought a house that was small and ugly, which needed a lot of repairs. They were both working hard on the floors in the kitchen of the house when her husband found a key to a door they hadn't noticed before. When he unlocked the door, they found stairs leading to an upper level of the home revealing a hidden room that was rich, ornate and beautifully decorated. She commented that, "It was such a happy surprise to find!"

In doing a quick review of this dream, at first this woman felt she was in a small and ugly place, a house or structure of her beliefs, working hard to repair her beliefs and make them better. Then her husband, who represents a very closely related action or idea she has embraced, found a key which unlocked something beautiful in her life. This closely related idea corresponds to her belief that being loved by her husband, and the action of being with him, surprisingly makes her feel vividly beautiful. She said that her husband holds the key to those beautiful parts of her, parts that she was unaware of. He has unlocked those beauties within her. When listening to the dreamer and how they feel about their dreams, the dream's most accurate message is often revealed.

Much like recurring dreams, there are recurring dilemmas or situations in life which appear to be repetitive.

By observing other people's experiences, insight concerning troubles that recur more often than would make sense for random occurrences will become apparent. For example, why do some people's difficulties seem to frequently reveal themselves in the area of health and wellness? Something distressing always seems to be happening to their body or to those with whom they love. Some people may find that their recurring dilemma is connected to financial security, or the finances of a loved one. Still others are continually unhappy because of hurt feelings due to loss of love, respect and approval. They often feel rejected, abused and deserted. Others are frustrated by a lack of expression, or attention, and find this experience as their greatest problem.

During a time of serious contemplation, a friend of mine came to an awareness of a personal recurring life dilemma. This dilemma was connected to associations with prominent men in her life. These men had a tendency to go from one job to another. The recurring situations began with her father, who was a used car salesman. She started her life observing an adult figure who never held down a steady job for more than a short time. He tried other means of employment, but usually went back to sell cars from one dealership to another, never truly finding success or happiness. He was always the dreamer, but never practical or aggressive in his goals, and he always thought that the "Grass was greener on the other side of the fence."

In her early twenties she married a man who, while going to college, changed his career choice several times, but eventually settled for a teaching degree. He landed several good teaching jobs, yet after a few years, he became disenchanted with each new job. Much like her father, he also felt the "Grass was greener on the other side of the fence." He ended up going from one teaching job to another. Even though they are now divorced and no longer engage in regular communication, she has heard through their children that he still struggles with his career.

Her present husband seems to have some of the same characteristics as the first two prominent men in her life. My friend has noticed a repeated job pattern in all of their lives; however, this repetition is something that involves her as well. One day, she asked herself, "Why do I keep seeing this picture manifesting in my closest male companions? What am I thinking or believing that keeps bringing about theses recurring dilemmas that effect my personal life situation?" By examining these repetitive situations as one would analyze a dream, my friend found a link that helped unlock the reasons for their recurrence, creating a shift in awareness which brought about a change in her life experience.

Recurrent dreams and repeating life experiences carry the same message to consciousness. The dreams and life experiences that repeat over a period of days, months, years, or sometimes throughout a lifetime, are certainly trying to reveal something that is not being received. These dreams and life experiences are not always identical with their circumstances or locations, but they most often reflect the same problem.

Recurring Flying Dreams

Dreamers who dream of flying see themselves as being free from the laws of the earth. If the flight is harmless and enjoyable, the dream is usually delightful. If the flight becomes dangerous, the dream takes on a more threatening tone. As a child, I often had dreams of flying, finding myself frequently running away from what I termed, 'A bad guy' who symbolized an action or idea that could cause pain or harm. In my dream, I would start running and then I would begin to fly. The faster my legs moved, the higher I would go. Sometimes I would fly far above the trees, and other times just high enough to avoid being caught by the 'bad guy'. These dreams usually occurred at times when I was presented with problems at school or was experiencing challenging situations in my personal life. All of us are trying to escape things that we are not yet ready to handle. Some flying dreams may be a type of escape and in some cases the flight may be a sort of reprieve, producing feelings of being invigorated, which can give strength in dealing with problems.

A man in his mid to late fifties had a brief flying dream with a profound message. He recalled being outside on a warm sunny day observing a strange occurrence in the sky, which at first glance appeared to be two birds fighting midair. Taking a closer look he noticed that the creature, a large bird with arms and hands, was juggling iron bars, catching them, throwing them high into the sky, catching them again while still flying. The bird creature was juggling successfully, but was flopping about flying with great difficulties. When the dreamer awakened, the first thought he had was, "Even though I am juggling things while flying, it might be easier to juggle things while on the ground." When I asked what he meant, he talked about how much he loves to daydream and occasionally finds his thoughts drifting while he should be focusing on more important matters.

This dreamer often experiences fun and exciting recurring flying dreams, but this dream changed his focus. He realized the difficulty of flying (daydreaming) while needing to do important tasks. These tasks felt like weights pulling him down, keeping him from enjoying his flight. He recognized that the tasks at hand needed to be performed while being grounded before he could experience the thrill and excitement of flying, his reprieve, which in the past allowed him to feel refreshed and strengthened.

When I was a little girl, I dreamed of seeing the world.
My mother would tell me to fly...fly into the sky and live my life.
So I flew, my eyes wide open, taking each
moment as a breath of fresh air.
One day I stopped and saw a little girl in prayer,
wishing she could spread her wings and fly as did I.
I saw a single tear slide down her cheek,
and looking closer I could see
that this little girl was me.
—C.A. Moore

Recurring Buried Alive Dreams

Dreaming of being buried alive may feel as if the earth is smothering life that is not ready to die! These dreams may reveal to the person that they need to address traits that are opposite to the one who dreams of flying. Some of the traits or attitudes that may need to be addressed and changed include the feeling of being burdened by acceptance of earth's limitations. They have accepted these burdens, but feel so smothered by them, that they cannot draw the breath of life or express themselves creatively. These belief systems were often formed early in life in an environment that made them feel over responsible. This person feels that they must always stay alert and tense to sense any dangers that may occur. All duties must be fulfilled and never refused.

Eventually these personalities feel overwhelmed and entombed by their heavy load. This challenge creates a feeling of hopelessness and defeat. They feel that they can never get ahead because of their many handicaps. They have excuses like, "I have no education and will never be able to get a good job," "I have no family support," "I am stupid." Feeling buried alive in work and despair, they sense no way out of their dilemma.

A recommended way out of overwhelming dilemmas is to find a means of developing the courage to take creative action based on the judgment of what would be best for all concerned, even if it means breaking habit patterns that seem permanent. One way to alter your belief system is to picture a different path. Motivational and inspirational teachers remind us that we can change our opinions about what we see, and the thing we have been seeing will change. Beliefs and life situations can be changed by adjusting negative feelings and visions, to those of joy and abundance. The following story is an example of how I created change in my personal belief system and life situation, by modifying the path that I kept seeing in my subconscious mind.

While attending a convention about personal transformation, I went to a class titled "Achieving Spiritual and Emotional Peace through Essential Oils" by Gary Young, founder of Young Living Essential Oils. Gary began the workshop by showing parts of a Walt Disney movie titled "Iron Will." There were several hundred in attendance filling the large ballroom at the Salt Palace Convention Center in Salt Lake City, Utah. Sitting in comfort and darkness, we waited for the movie to begin.

The first scene revealed a young teenage boy and his father riding dog sleds through the snow. We watched with anxiety as the boy's father fell into a lake of ice, and died. At this point in the movie, Gary stopped the clip and encouraged us to write down the first words that came to mind. He repeated this process by showing more clips of the movie while we continued to write down our inward thoughts. It wasn't long before my tears began to flow in acknowledgement of inner thoughts that were less than positive; thoughts filled with doubt and images of pain.

Crying and trying to gain some sense of composure, I felt a strong presence nearby. Standing in front of me, patiently waiting to be noticed was Gary! Out of the hundreds of people in attendance at the workshop, I was surprised to see him standing there! He handed me a bottle of an essential oil blend, which I gladly used, then he walked away. Rubbing my hands together and cupping them over my face, I took a deep, healing breath. Experiencing a feeling of comfort and peace, I was able to continue with the experience unruffled, relaxed, and with more clarity.

After the movie and the awareness exercise, Gary talked to us about breaking down our "Wall of Terror." I had an intimate "Wall of Terror" and had sensed it for years. It stopped me from progressing, from making choices that were for my highest good. My journey seemed too difficult, the wall massively thick and strong. I was tormented with too much pain to get past that wall!

Coming home from the convention I decided to tackle this "Wall of Terror." Developing the courage to change, and using essential oils for emotional support, I imagined the destruction of my brick wall. High quality therapeutic grade essential oils are vital when dealing with emotional issues. They can be uplifting, protective, calming, and are molecularly aligned to specific responses in the human body. It was with the intention of achieving a specific response, the destruction of my "Wall of Terror," that I began punching it down. I envisioned smashing a hole through the middle of the wall. POW! BAM! CRASH! An opening began to form showing through to the other side. For a week I kept punching at this wall, seeing past the hole to a different pathway. Then one day spirit said, "Laina, you can stop punching now. It's time to walk through the opening. You tore down the wall on the first day. It's time to use your courage, be brave and step through the opening."

While smelling essential oils that supported feelings of calmness and courage, I imagined myself walking through the hole in my intimate "Wall of Terror." When, through the hole to the other side, several paths appeared. Taking time to analyze the assorted pathways, and after several days of confusion, I realized that the path of most focus was one built from scar tissue and pain. Bumpy low rolling hills made from a creamy, yellow substance, which looked similar to scar tissue you would find in the human body, could be seen for miles. The route between the hills was riddled with twisting vines created from pain and agony. The road was bulging with these vines and every step taken filled my soul with anguish! This was the path I had been walking, the path on the other side of my "Wall of Terror." No wonder I was afraid to walk through the wall! Even though I overcame my fear by breaking through the wall, the only path I saw and was familiar with was one of pain. By realizing that the painful path was in my past, I prayed to know what to do next.

During an early morning prayer walk, I recognized that the way to change the path of most focus was to envision a different one. The impression to visualize a new course in life was an answer to my prayers. Having the courage to take creative action was a progressive and beneficial activity necessary to make important life changing adjustments. This new path needed to be something visual, something without scars or bumps or images of agonizing pain.

Using positive self talk, I recited the following: "I live a life of joy, peace, security and abundance." One day, I paid special attention to what my feelings were while repeating those words. To my utter amazement, what I really felt and heard was, "I live a life of stress and fear!" The spoken positive words were not strong enough to make a difference!

What needed to be done was to mentally and emotionally design a different path. To do this I found three people who would be good mentors and with their support, I was able to set personal, spiritual, and business goals. This action plan seemed to work because my feelings began to alter from hopelessness, stress and fear, to excitement, anticipation and faith.

While on another prayer walk, I had a new thought. "What if I found a picture of a path that was beautiful and comforting, and looked at it daily until my internal path vision changed? I often do that with objects such as jewelry, cars, clothing, and other tangible things. Why not use that same process for visualizing a new path?" While smelling essential oils that vibrated creativity and joy, I searched for pictures and photos of beautiful pathways. It wasn't long before a pleasant and comfortable path image appeared. This path surrounded a clear, blue lake and was gently situated in a lush, green valley. The picture of tall pine trees, ducks, geese, small animals and birds, with a flat and gentle dirt trail that meandered around the lake, filled my heart and internal sight with peaceful pleasure.

Not only did an emotionally supportive path appear, I found several others as well. Depending on my mood, I can visit a mountain path, garden path, a sandy beach path, or other inviting and comforting paths. They are all filled with beauty and pleasure, not pain and scar tissue. Now, with every step I take, there is beauty! With a new life design and path pictures, there is expectancy for a brighter future, one less scarred and painful.

Soon, after changing my path, I had a dream where I gave birth to a new child. This was an encouraging message. Often when there are dreams of giving birth, the dreamer is sensing a new life within taking place, the birth of a new action, idea, feeling or emotion. The dream was a message revealing success because I changed my path through courageous actions!

Recurring Falling Dreams

Dreams often reveal our personalities. Falling dreams can reveal personalities that are usually pleasing with better than an average ability to make a positive first impression. They can be somewhat self-critical in areas they like to keep private. They may often hear self talk such as, "They won't like you as much when they find out what you are really like." With these feelings about their inner faults, they have uncertainty in regard to new contacts, making the relationship feel insecure and uncertain.

With confidence in their ability to make a good first impression, fear can encroach in their ability to develop a closer relationship. Keeping casual friends seems to be their forte while developing long lasting friendships is often avoided. If this habit grows in the individual, feelings of insecurity also increase. Boasting for approval and flattering others may begin to take place. As time goes on, the feeling of insecurity and unsure footing becomes more prevalent, with the falling dream becoming more frightening, much like a nightmare.

There are also personalities of high achievers that experience similar feelings of insecurity and unsure footing. Even though these personalities often present themselves as extremely confident and capable, they may occasionally experience thoughts of uncertainty and hesitation. One of my daughters had intermittent dreams of falling. For several years, she was a single mother working three jobs. One of her jobs was extremely demanding where she was expected to do certain tasks without training. Because she is a very self motivated person, she would focus her attention to figure out the proper procedure of getting the task completed. This didn't happen without her experiencing feelings of inadequacy and fear, which manifested dreams of falling. Realizing the dreams held a message about how she was feeling concerning work, she would mentally and emotionally push through the learning process until she learned how to do the job, while at the same time knowing she was acquiring a new and valuable skill. She knew that the falling dreams would subside once she felt competent in her new abilities.

People who experience dreams of falling must find a way to descend safely and consciously from the precarious position which they have taken. By understanding the message in the falling dreams, the dreamer can begin to choose a better way, one without false pretenses. They can display actions stemming from a new awareness of their intentions. As soon as the dreamer begins to show the actions, even if the activity is small, they will begin to see the myths in the methods or thoughts they once used. This new awareness will give them the capability to expose some of their faults, as well as strengths, and they will quickly discover that their path is not as difficult or painful as it had once seemed to be.

Recurring Fire Dreams

Fire, which is often referred to by ancient philosophers as one of the four elements, is frequently connected to passionate feelings, something that gives warmth, or a component that is too hot and wild to manage. It is often spoken of as a type of cleansing element associated with burning. When we hear the word 'fire' certain emotions and words come to mind such as heat, pressure, pain, pleasure, passion, creativity, warmth, contentment or danger. It is in the home where we use fire to cook our food and warm the heart, and it is fire that can also destroy the home and its comforts!

Fire has been associated with purification, the burning out of the unusable and undesirable, as well as deep anger and self-loathing. Dreaming of our homes or possessions being threatened by fire would represent the dissolving of old forms, old places of dwelling, our structure of beliefs.

There is a widely circulated story around a scripture in the Bible. The story begins with a group of women who are discussing Malachi 3:3, "And he shall sit as a refiner and purifier of silver; and he shall purify the sons of Levi, and purge them as gold and silver, that they may offer unto the Lord an offering in righteousness." The women wonder what this scripture means, particularly the statement, "He shall sit as a refiner and purifier of silver." One of the women in the group offers to learn about the process of refining silver and get back to the group with her findings at the next Bible study.

The woman sets an appointment with a silversmith, never mentioning anything about the reason for her visit, only her curiosity about the process of refining silver. As she watches the silversmith, he holds a piece of silver over the fire and allows it to heat up. He explains that in refining silver, a person needs to hold the silver in the middle of the fire where the flames are hottest to burn away all the impurities. The woman imagines God holding us in such a hot spot; then she thinks again about the verse that says,

"He sits as a refiner and purifier of silver." She asks the silversmith if it is true that he has to sit in front of the fire the whole time. The man answers, "Yes. Not only do I need to sit here holding the silver, but I have to keep my eyes on the silver the entire time it is in the fire. If the silver is left a moment too long in the flames, it will be destroyed." The woman is silent for a moment, then asks, "How do you know when the silver is fully refined?" The man smiles at her and answers, "Oh that's easy, it is refined when I see my image in it."

When feeling the heat of the fire in life, fires that may be showing up in dreams, remember that God is there watching. He is near the fire assisting with the internal purification, always keeping watch until he sees his image in the cleansing process and the job is complete.

Recurring Insufficient Clothing Dreams

A person is likely to dream of being without sufficient clothing if they feel that they are, for whatever reason, constantly embarrassing themselves or others. They may lack the social skills to be pleasant, or they may lack the ability to be reserved in the amount of information they share. The recurrence of an unclothed dream may indicate that a person feels it's time to incorporate some agreeable social habits with more pleasant manners. They are beginning to feel the need to graciously assert their right to decent privacy, to defend themselves against rude or point blank questions, and set personal boundaries.

Learning how to set a personal boundary is a learned skill which can be done with grace and charm. Once a person realizes that setting boundaries is an option in bringing them happiness, they will begin to refrain from jumping into situations that make them feel vulnerable. They will start to express appropriate first impressions and become more reserved in their social habits.

While participating in a dream healing project using essential oils, flower essences, music, various healing stones and crystals, I experienced an intriguing insufficient clothing dream. The intention of the dream healing project was to stimulate dreams with messages. Each night before bed, I used specific essential oils, either applied topically to my body or diffused through the air. I also listened to music that had been chosen for its association to a specific emotion. It was early in the project while I was using my oils and listening to music of a mystical, melancholy nature, that I had an insufficient clothing dream.

The dream began at a school function with my husband, who was a school teacher, and me. I was lost and only partially dressed. As I looked around I found a T-shirt that I could purchase to cover myself, only I realized that I had no money. I proceeded to pick up a T-shirt and at once felt I should steal the shirt, but put it down instead. In the next moment, I noticed that I was wearing the shirt, but I was still lost. I saw another person who looked lost, but she was not lost. I asked to use her cell phone only to discover that I couldn't figure out how to call my husband to come rescue me. A man came over and told me that I couldn't dial long distance. All the people in town had prepaid phones for local calls only. I decided to call my ex-mother-in-law because I was in her city. When I reached her on the phone, I began to cry as I told her how I stole a T-shirt and was lost. After gaining some composure, I asked her to call my husband to come and take me home.

When I awoke from this dream, I immediately realized that I needed to assert my right to privacy during this dream experiment and stop expressing myself so freely. The key symbols in the dream which brought me to this awareness were: my husband—who represented closely related actions and ideas, the school—which represented a place of learning, the lost woman—who represented feelings and emotions I thought I had lost within myself, and my ex-mother-in-law—who reminded me of closely related feelings and emotions I had often experienced in the past. By realizing the dream message of needing privacy, I began to graciously set personal boundaries and soon felt much happier and less vulnerable. I had a successful experience with the dream experiment and gained some valuable insight into my feelings, emotions, and beliefs.

Recurring Water Dreams

Water is the original element from which all forms of life have come. Water is often related to the dreamer's emotional life. It can represent the great unconscious where all ideas, emotions and behaviors spring. The form the water takes in our dreams, and our relationship to it, can determine what the unconscious is trying to reveal.

Dreams of water that involve finding a cool spring and drinking to quench a deep thirst can be pleasant, with pleasing significance. The discovery of the deep springs within, springs that can relieve tensions and quench the thirst for understanding, may revealed. Sparkling running waters could be symbolic of distinct living and moving places within the unconscious. They may depict natural instincts and desires that come freely to consciousness finding acceptable expression.

Dreams of resting peacefully with the calm swaying movement of the ocean can bring comfort and peace leaving the dreamer feeling restored and serene. This type of dream could be revealing the inner happiness and contentment of the dreamer. These dreams often follow periods of striving for accomplishment when the person has come to a well-earned rest.

In dreams where the water is rough, dark, swampy and full of obstacles, feelings of fearful attachments may be revealing themselves. The dreamer could be in a fretful, complaining, and whining place as they are attempting to fix their emotions and release to a better place. This dream often represents an important transitional period with the need for removal from a difficult situation. Movement is necessary to get rid of the stagnation and fixation they find themselves stuck in.

A young man I know has many recurring water dreams. One of his dreams found him with his wife and daughters in his grandparents' home. He wasn't sure why he was there. Looking around, he observed water that was building up outside the house. It began to seep through the cracks around the door, leaking into the home. As he noticed this dilemma, he told himself, "Okay, I need to clean this place. When I am ready, I am going to open the doors and let the water inside to do the cleaning." He opened the doors, the water rushed through the house, knocking over his little daughter whom he quickly rescued, and left the carpets and surrounding areas saturated with the water. He began to clean up the wet residue, then woke up.

I asked the dreamer about the condition of the outside water. He mentioned that it was only slightly dirty, not filthy. He needed to let the water into the house to assist with the cleaning. By allowing this water in, which symbolized a flood of emotions, he would be able to clean his structure of beliefs, represented by his grandparents' home, a place to the young man which symbolized goodness and comfort. Even though his tender feelings and emotions, typified by his little daughter, were knocked over in the cleaning, no harm was done. He said that there was still some work to be done, some sucking up of the water, or cleansing of his emotions, but he felt confident that the work could be completed. As we discussed the dream, he was able to see the message that revealed a personal desire to do some internal emotional cleaning.

In a previous water dream, the young man, his wife, their two little girls, his sister and bother-in-law with their three daughters, were surfing on a beautiful, sandy beach. He mentioned that he did a surfing technique which was different from most surfing techniques; this style of surfing took the person across the shore in an instant. After he did the trick, he found himself at the other end of the shoreline where he began to do some gold panning. While gold panning, he discovered a solid gold chain! In his excitement, he asked his brother-in-law to help him retrieve the chain, because the majority of the chain was buried in the sand. They pulled on the chain, which eventually revealed a solid gold statue of a woman resembling something you would see on the front of an old pirate ship. The two young men cashed in their treasure and became so wealthy that they bought the shore they surfed on, the same shore where they found the statue. They lived in a house on the shore while they continued looking for more gold. The young father exclaimed, "I was really, really rich."

As we begin to analyze this dream, the first thing we need to know is what water means to the dreamer, and in this situation, water means "life." At the time of the dream, the young man was in a state of transition from one job, having just finished a certification program, to being unemployed seeking a better, more enjoyable profession. He told me that in his waking hours, all he thinks about is making a lot of money, while seeking fun ways to accomplish those desires. He wants to find the key, the 'trick' that would allow him to make the money he daily imagines himself enjoying, while experiencing pleasure in what he does to provide a living. This dream appears to be a genuine manifestation of his desires related to his emotional life, a life he is now ready to manifest which includes great wealth and enjoyment.

As we can see by the two water dream examples, this young man is often given messages from his subconscious concerning his emotions. These are personal messages filled with guidance which he uses to develop and improve himself while adjusting his belief structure. Because he is aware that there are messages in his dreams, he looks for those communications. By making subtle life adjustments, his vision becomes clearer, his path more certain and his life more serene.

When observing that a dream or life experience is recurring, pay attention and ask to understand the message that source is trying to convey. Once you become aware of the messages being delivered, and gain an understanding of what the subconscious is trying to teach, knowledge can be received that will unlock mysteries and influence a change in your life path. Change can be created by using wisdom revealed in dreams.

Night
—By Paul Laurence Dunbar

Silence, and whirling worlds afar
Through all encircling skies.
What floods come o'er the spirits bar,
What wondrousness thoughts arise.

The earth, a mantle falls away,
And, winged, we leave the sod;
Where shines in its eternal sway
The Majesty of God.

Chapter 4

The Communication Mystery

"It is not in the stars to hold our destiny but in ourselves"
—William Shakespeare

The unconscious is generally not verbal. There are times in dreams when words are used, but even those words may have symbolic meanings. Remember that dreams are allegories or parables; realize that dreams are telling stories with masked meanings. Time and thought must be taken to untangle the significance of the dream symbols before the story can reveal its emotion filled message.

The unconscious is symbolically revealing the emotions which are affecting our lives, whether positive or negative. These feelings are hiding behind blind spots working without supervision or control. The mind chooses the symbols that best represent these emotions. Ingenuity must be used at times to reveal painful feelings so that the dreamer can receive these messages in a way that is bearable. The conscious mind has determined that certain words and symbols stand for specific emotions that can act as triggers which release a current of feelings circling around a particular idea or picture.

Understanding the emotional vocabulary that will enable the dreamer to interpret dreams is worth patient effort. Feelings and words make an image that acts as a link between the conscious and unconscious, between the daily living and the dream world. In the dream the feeling creates the picture which is the dream story. Thinking about the dream and its symbolic meaning translates it into understandable words and then dreams that once seemed strange and unusual begin to make sense.

In attempting to understand dreams and their emotional messages, remember to use the dreamer's emotional experience in relation with the symbols. A particular symbol may carry a special meaning that could not apply to the life experiences and situations of anyone else. In the following sections, you will learn some basic symbols and their possible meanings. There will be as many variations of a symbol's meanings as there are people. Different people will choose various symbols to depict the same emotion. That variation is important in interpreting dreams, because that symbol indicates the association which that particular emotion has for the dreamer. A symbol that may appear abstract to one person can in reality represent something very tangible to another. Therefore, symbolic representations defined in this book are only suggestions to stimulate thought.

Key Symbols and Words

Coins: Coins symbolize a small portable token of exchange, an earned reward or gift. To some, coins represent power, prosperity, a change in life habits, or opportunities. When misplaced or thrown out, they may represent loss. Yet to other people, coins may be symbolic of wealth and values.

A man once had a dream where he was doing construction work at a house owned by a woman. While working on this house, he noticed a display case full of valuables and coins, worth much money. Knowing that the display case was going to be left behind when the woman sold the house, the man dared to ask the woman if she would consider selling the case and its contents. She agreed to sell it to him for fifty dollars. He happily paid the money and instantly found himself extremely prosperous. During his life, the man had considered himself poor and uneducated; however in the dream, his knowledge about things of value, along with his courageous actions to acquire them, brought him great unexpected wealth. When taking this message to heart the man began to realize that by using courageous action in areas that he valued, there were many important opportunities for wealth and success in his life.

In contrast, the stealing of coins in dreams reveals the unconscious beliefs that undervalue the self. Like the Judas story in the Bible where he sold out Christ for thirty pieces of silver. This person possibly feels that they must clutch at the little values and approval of others rather than explore the depths of their own inner wealth.

Colors: Dreaming of colors can be significant and indicate another facet to the dream. For example, if the dreamer sees a blue hat, the color blue may have as much symbolism as the hat. Blue is often associated with thoughts and ideas of comfort and peace. Find out what the specific color represents to the dreamer.

Death: Death can represent many different emotions such as sorrow, dissolution, disappointments, bad news, the end of a phase in life, transitions, or closure. To assist the dreamer in understanding this type of dream, it is important to learn what the dreamer is experiencing in life at the time of a death dream.

Earth: Earth is the worldly foundation that often represents security. It may symbolize the foundation of facts or material possessions on which to build a life. It is the ground under the structures of thought. The earth is the mother of all creation that gives sustenance. A dream where the land breaks into great crevices opening at one's feet is an example of the unconscious feeling that the earthly security is failing. It is more likely to appear in dreams when lifelong values are proving to be unreliable. An example could be when financial institutions collapse and permanent retirement programs and savings are lost.

"The Earth does not belong to man; Man belongs to the Earth.
This we know. All things are connected like
the blood which unites one family.
Whatever befalls the Earth befalls the sons of the Earth.
Man did not weave the web of life, he is merely a strand in it.
Whatever he does to the web, he does to himself."
—Chief Seattle

House or Dwelling: Our houses or dwellings, no matter how large or small, ornate or simple, have been to humankind a place of refuge, protection, security, privacy, and comfort. They represent a place where we are intimate with our closest companions, a place where we can relax and be ourselves protected from the outside world. A man's house has always been his castle, to be defended and cared for with all his might! In like manner, we defend and care for the structure of thoughts, beliefs, and feelings in which we live and move. Our present affairs or current belief structure, which is part of our physical being, is often symbolized in dreams by images of a house or dwelling. It is primarily composed of the results of our own personal life occurrences involving thinking, feeling, sensing and intuitive moments.

In preparing to write this book, I read numerous publications, listened to many lectures and several talks about dreams, the subconscious mind, and human psychology. After two weeks of constant research about dreams, I had a curious dream. I found myself in a beautiful house, which was fairly large and nicely built. At the beginning of the dream I had met a young woman with a little girl named Enchantress. This young woman and her daughter needed a place to stay for a short time, so I invited them to stay in my home. One day, while working in the back room of my house, with my children playing by my side, we discovered that the furniture in the home was quite elegant. We were new to the home and hadn't uncovered the furniture, which was carefully protected with blankets.

The scene changed and I entered my kitchen, where

I discovered that this young woman and her daughter Enchantress had moved in all their belongings and completely took over my home. She had music blasting, plus all her family were there laughing and being noisy. I couldn't concentrate to work on my book because of the noise, nor could I cook because she had taken over the kitchen area. I went to the rear workroom and spoke with my children. We all voiced feelings of frustration because we felt trapped in the back room, unable to do anything in our own home. After talking with my children, I went out to the room where the young lady was standing, but I couldn't see! My eyes were shut and I couldn't open them. I yelled, "I can't handle this! I can't stand having this many people here. Y'all have to leave! Sorry, but this is not going to work out. You need to leave my house now!" After ranting I regained my ability to see and I noticed that the girl and her family appeared intensely hurt when I told them to leave. Then I proceeded to go back into the workroom for a few minutes and found when I came out a short while later, the young woman and her family had removed all her belongings and left.

As we look at this dream subjectively, by studying my feelings about the images in the dream, we can pick up on an interesting message. My home represented the development of a new structure of beliefs gleaned from the studies I had been researching. All of this new information felt enthralling (enchanting) at first, as I invited it into my structure of beliefs. The symbols represented by the young woman, her daughter and their family, were my new actions, ideas, feelings and emotions which were causing me to feel overwhelmed. Fresh ideas converged with existing ones and my belief system began to sense an overload creating frustration and anxiety with an inability to see what to do next. It was time to clear out the new structure so that I could work peacefully. I decided to stop my research and allow myself time to digest what I had recently learned. The awareness of needing to assimilate the new information was represented by the kitchen scene in the dream, the kitchen I wasn't able to use because of too much stuff! My mind cleared after a few days and I felt the distracting emotions leave. I was was able to continue my work and research.

Moon: Many people think of the moon as the cool, reflected light of night, as changeable as a woman, a symbol of life, death and rebirth, a time of measurement for planting, harvesting and fertility. In some instances it represents success in love and the presence of wealth. The moon has been a powerful symbol in our collective feelings for centuries with songs and stories written about it. It has been worshipped as a goddess and couples have fallen in love under its influence. The moon will have a special meaning according to individual and personal experiences with it.

I spoke with a man who had an interesting dream about the moon, with a personal and intriguing meaning for the moon symbol. In his dream, there were two moons. These moons were both visible during the day as well as the night. The dream scene began during the daytime where the two moons were first revealed. One of the moons was in half moon shape; the other moon was full and smaller. It was because of their size differences that an awareness of the existence of the two moons began. The dreamer, as well as the people present in the dream, hadn't noticed the moons before. Everyone in the local area was trying to decide if the smaller moon was an illusion. They decided to consult experts to learn if the two moons were an optical illusion or anything factual. The reason for looking at the moon in the first place was to decide if there was any type of nourishment available on the moon. Having two moons seemed radically outlandish. The dreamer thought, "There probably wasn't any food on the one moon anyway."

When I asked the dreamer what the moon symbolized to him, he thought a moment, and said "nourishment." I didn't personally think that would be something the moon would symbolize, but he did and it was very symbolic for him. As we continued to analyze the dream and its symbols, he told me that the moon has a steady effect on our world, "It influences the tides, the growing seasons, our entire planet and its functions. It helps to sustain our life here on the earth."

> *"Spectral in heaven as climbs the*
> *frail veiled moon, so climbs my dream."*
> —William Rose Benét

Rain: Regardless of language and nationality, people have all experienced rain to some extent. This one word may have many connections. It has common meanings of nourishment, pleasure, wetness, plant growth, prosperity, life, alarm, bliss, survival, quenching of thirst, and even heaven's tears. It has been felt, seen, heard, smelled and tasted. The emotions that are connected to rain may differ according to each individual's personal experience. For example, if a person experiences a major crisis during a rainstorm, often when a rainstorm occurs thereafter, similar painful emotions may be triggered.

Soil: Dry and arid soil could represent an undeveloped state of one's possibilities where latent powers, not watered by the rich unconscious, could grow and flourish. Rich, fertile soil could represent the well-used riches of potential and the bearing of the fruit of one's labors. Soil rich in minerals and ores could represent principles of integrity and natural resources basic in nature and the individual.

Sun: This word may release a variety of emotional feelings depending on the dreamer's experiences. There are several feelings and thoughts associated with this word, some of which are the desert, discomfort, heat, light, life, rest, relaxation, sunburn, suntan, sunstroke, summer, thirst, prosperity, delight, and warmth from its rays.

Teeth: Teeth are structures whose typical function is to break down food. In dreams this symbol could easily stand for the body bringing to the dreamer's conscious awareness, the need to address unknown dental problems or sickness. Dreams are often used to diagnose certain maladies; however, a more symbolic meaning of teeth dreams could be the representation of the dreamer's ability to analyze and break down thoughts concerning feelings about life and circumstances.

By sharing my feelings and talking with my family or friends about a subject that is bothering me, I receive clarity. Sometimes in analyzing certain conditions, I discuss the matter until I can no longer stand to talk about it. When this happens, I often have a dream where every time I try to speak, my teeth start falling out of my mouth. I spew out teeth like a spitting grasshopper! I wake up knowing that I am done examining the situation and realize it's time to move on.

A disturbing tooth dream was shared by one of my relatives who was going through a difficult transition period in his life. Just graduating from college, he was struggling to find a job to support his wife and children. One night, he had a dream where he felt something in his teeth near his gums. As he began to pull on a string, bigger than dental floss, strong and tough like sinew, his gums began to hurt, yet the string never stopped coming! He said, "There were tons of this string, it had no end! It was very painful. Finally I had to cut it."

The dreamer associated his teeth and gums with his mouth. He mentioned that without his mouth, he had no way to eat or sustain life and he felt that he had no voice. He found that his present state of unemployment, and his need to find a way to take care of his family, was very stressful and painful. The string which was causing him so much pain seemed never ending and very strong, not at all pliable, much like his employment status. He saw no end to the string and no resolution to his unemployment predicament.

The Cross: In many religions over the years, the cross has symbolized surrendering of selfish and egotistical desires and ambitions. To Christians, it often represents the sacrifice made by Jesus for the good of mankind. The saying, "Take up your cross," represents accepting the problems or difficulties in which one may find themselves by discovering inner resources to solve the problem.

Another meaning of the cross may be to 'cross out' the old habits and ideas which are deceptive and embrace empowering convictions and actions that come from the creative center. Carrying a cross of self-pity can be a heavy burden. By throwing off crosses, or personal burdens, the dreamer can proceed with courage and power to enjoy a more fulfilled life.

The Crown and Scepter: The crown is a symbol of royalty, authority, earthly heritage, unusual privileges, worthiness, political desires, and recognition for outstanding abilities. A crown could take the shape of a laurel wreath, a crown of thorns, an attractive tiara or a heavy jeweled crown which could represent too much responsibility. In whatever appearance the crown takes, it forms a bridge to feelings in relation to ruler-ship or achievements.

The scepter can symbolize sovereignty or authority and can present itself in the forms of a slave driver's whip bringing pain and torment, or a musical conductor's baton, bringing harmony and agreement to relationships.

Water: This symbolizes the great reservoir of the unconscious which affects behaviors and emotions, and may be linked to the amniotic fluid we lived in while inside the womb. The meaning of water varies depending on the form it appears in the dream and our relationship to it. The following are some possible water symbols and what they may represent to the dreamer.

Drowning

Since water often represents the great unconscious where all ideas, emotions, and actions spring, recurring dreams of drowning may be experienced. These dreams can bring the dreamer to an awareness of thoughts and feelings they are having of being overwhelmed with tasks, loss, emotions, and responsibilities. The dreamer often feels that they are barely able to keep their head above water. The following is an example of a dream my mother had which came during a difficult transitional time in her life. She also includes her personal interpretation:

"I dreamed about my brother-in-law. I was telling him off, putting him in his place. Then my granddaughter slipped into a tiny creek of water that became big water. She managed to half float while barely keeping her head above water. Her dad, who was also my brother-in-law, jumped in to save her, but only went to the top of creek. He took a very long time, I seemed unconcerned. Then I came back and he had her in his arms wrapped up. I asked how she was, and he said she was okay. Each of the people in the dream including the drowning granddaughter represented me. At the time of the dream I felt like I was drowning with all my life choices and challenges. Because of the dream message, I received a new awareness about my situation, got help, and was okay, but it took a while."

Floods

Dreams of floods and rivers overflowing with melting ice and snow could represent the releasing of frozen concepts and emotional stiffness. These types of dreams can be somewhat frightening as the dreamer begins to release their long held emotions of superiority and satisfaction. In some flood dreams, homes are carried away by strong currents of water and destroyed or relocated in unfamiliar places. This may represent a person's structure of beliefs being swept away.

A man who had recently acquired a new job had a flood dream which revealed his strong emotional connection to his employment. In the dream, his home, which was a manufactured home, was 'uprooted' by a flood and placed somewhere else. The home was put in a place unfamiliar to him, surrounded by people he didn't know. At the end of the dream, the house became secure and the trauma passed.

I asked the dreamer what was going on in his life when the dream occurred. Because of a subtle comment his boss made to him about his work performance, he felt impressed that his boss may not keep him around very long. This disturbed him and he likened the dream to his feelings about his new job, feelings of insecurity and weakness for not knowing his job duties very well. Emotionally he didn't feel strongly rooted or secure in his new position, which was represented by the manufactured home being so easily swept away in a flood because of a weak foundation.

After understanding the dream symbols and their meanings, plus the emotion he experienced at having a dream with a good ending, the man felt confident that the job situation would have a good resolve. This added boost of confidence helped him at work. At last contact, the man was still employed there and was learning how to deal with his boss with less fear.

Life in Water

Bodies of water teaming with fish are symbolic of the productivity of the unconscious mind, often representing a healthy emotional life full of family and close friends. Fish, as living organisms that grow within the water, could also represent the living and growing ideas of the dreamer. Dreaming about gathering fish in great quantities could represent an abundance of ideas, as with one who is 'fishing for ideas'. If the fish represent creatures of harm, the dream is warning about having or consuming emotions that may have suppressed negative beliefs.

A fish dream could come to someone who is trying to achieve great deeds in a hurry. In rushing into this endeavor they may feel tense and uptight. This type of dream could take place in the ocean where the dreamer is trying to land a whale (a whale of a project, a whale of an idea, a whale of a problem), feeling overwhelmed and exhausted. The dreamer may hang on to the whale with all their strength and wake up feeling fatigued. With this type of dream, the symbolic message can be that some things require patience, while taking small steps with consistent effort.

Tidal Waves

Tidal waves, or what is officially termed Tsunami's, are a series of larger than normal waves, waves that, at first glance, look like a rapidly rising tide. These waves are caused from earthquakes, volcanic eruptions or underwater explosions. The underwater disruption is necessary for a new adjustment on the earth's surface, with a need to restore balance between land and water. A tidal wave dream may indicate the need to restore a balance between feelings and emotions the dreamer has experienced or buried. These occurrences and beliefs need to be assimilated and brought to awareness in consciousness.

A young family was living in an extremely small isolated community when one of their teenage daughters had a traumatic tidal wave dream. In her dream, the teenager found herself outside with her family, where everyone was waiting for a tidal wave to strike land. The young teenager told me how each person braced for the wave. Then she said, "When it came, I felt it 'punch' with great force. There was intense cold and horrifying blackness. Once the wave hit, I was able to float to the top of the water, but I was away from my family. It was horrifying!"

During the interpretation of the dream, the young girl realized that being outside was not a place of protection or safety, as being in a building or home would have been. Outside represented a place isolated from the rest of the world where she felt vulnerable to life's elements. Her family, which represented her closely related feelings, emotions, actions and ideas, symbolized her fears and beliefs of feeling helpless toward the dangers that were coming.

While assisting the dreamer in understanding the dream message, the young girl realized that life, with its difficult changes, her feelings of danger, darkness and loneliness, was manifested through the tidal wave dream.

She learned that she would survive the challenges she faced. By realizing that her soul language was manifesting a message of survival, she was able to find balance with an increased awareness that she would get through her painful experiences. The young woman has frequent recurring water dreams. Through interpreting her dreams, she has learned that recurring water dreams are messages revealing her emotional state.

Our dreams are often our subconscious mind giving us hints about things that we need to change or take note of. When they occur to the point that we notice that they are reoccurring, we may have missed the point the first, second or third time. So, pay attention! Our conscious thoughts are only a small part of our enormous brain power.

Chapter 5

Through the Eyes of a Child

"Up anchor! Up anchor!
Set sail and away!
The ventures of dreamland
Are thine for a day."
—Silas Weir Mitchell

*P*arents should encourage children to share their dreams. Dreams are an expression of the child's emotional problems and can become a valuable source of information to the parents. It is not necessary to share the interpretation of the dream with the child. The information gleaned from a child's dream should be used by the parent to find ways toward understanding and helping the child solve their problems. By stating brief comments such as, "Sounds like you are worried about something" or, "You sound hurt" or, "Is there any trouble at school that is bothering you?" an atmosphere for discussion may be created which can be helpful to both the parent and the child.

Another thing to consider when interpreting a child's dream is the mood in which they went to sleep. To a child, sleep sometimes seems like going away, a type of separation from the mother. Occasionally this feeling of separation creates a great loneliness or fear to the child, so they often resist sleep. The night seems like a lifetime of detachment from the exciting daily activities and their connection to mother. Knowing this, parents can find ways to make the last contact of the day between them and their children pleasant and reassuring. Connect the night separation and the morning reunion by a loving reassurance that mother will be there. Help them to feel that an unseen loving presence will always be there to protect them. My mother often told me that I had a guardian angel and that if I were ever afraid, I could call upon my angel for protection. This brought comfort through childhood and continued to be with me through difficult times as I grew older.

When a child grows into adolescence, consider the life problems of this age. The child is emerging from the influences of the home and parental approval to the agreement of the crowd and their peers. In this growth process, children may attempt to balance their own insecurities with disapproval and judgment of others. This can make a child feel exposed and criticized because they know other adolescents are doing the same thing to them. If adults remark on the child's appearance, height or weight and conduct, these experiences, along with those of their peers, may express themselves in dreams as being exposed or improperly dressed in public. If a child dreamed they were barefoot in a place where they should have been wearing shoes, this could be interpreted by realizing the function of the shoes, which could symbolize protection from earth contacts. They may be feeling a lack of experience in social skills or the absence of a helpful philosophy of life.

In adolescence there will be dreams of professional choices, sex, romance, fears and feelings of inadequacy, a struggle to find independence and a search to find acceptance with others not connected to family. This age is a time when children are beginning an emotional break from family into adulthood, which can be very difficult. Their dreams will contain symbols which represent these various conflicts. By simply asking for the associations, the connections can be seen.

Listed below are some dream symbols that may manifest in a child's dream. Remember to ask the child what a particular symbol represents to them before proceeding with the dream interpretation.

Children's Dream Symbols

Angels: Angels may be ideas in the service of God, protectors, messengers, comforters, guardians.

Animals: As with all animals in a child's dream, find out what the particular animal represents to them. A little girl once had a dream about penguins and black bears. She told me that there were one thousand black bears and one thousand penguins. "The penguins were not real; they were full of live fish." She and her friends gathered up all the penguins. Someone noticed a crack in a penguin. They opened up all the penguins and dumped the fish into the bear's mouths. They fed all the fish to the bears. Then all the children played a game running in circles like a dragon. There were some friends who chose to tell the truth and some friends chose a dare. Then the children circled the pond and one thousand bears got fish while the girls jumped to the other side of the pond like dragons. Since they all dared, the little girl said she had to do it too. "The coach got us," she said. The coach was her mother.

After asking the little girl what each symbol meant, we were able to see a message in her dream. Peer pressure was becoming evident in her life as she grew into adolescence. By feeding the desires of belonging and the need to feel included with her friends, she was beginning to realize there were dangers involved. Amidst the dangers, she relied on her mother's assistance, who was her coach to help her get through her exciting and scary experiences and situations. Understanding this dream encouraged the mother to help her child deal with future peer pressure.

Elves: They are often represented as problem solvers or actions towards others that are good and helpful such as healing and fixing.

Fairies: These may symbolize ideas and feelings which are original and new. If the fairies are kind, they may represent kind ideas, magic, a favorable omen, and abundance. If the fairies are wicked, they could represent unkind and disagreeable ideas and even a sense of lack.

Not only do children dream of fairies, but on occasion young adults and adults may enjoy their dream presence too. A young adult woman related a dream to me that began one morning after she woke early to the sound of her phone. She had to set the alarm so she could attend a conference at some wetlands forty-five minutes north of a large city. The hosts were leading a nature walk and offered breakfast to those who were their guests. She knew she had a long day and that more sleep would be necessary, so she fell back asleep. She said that as she fell back to sleep, she experienced a lucid dream. A lucid dream is any dream in which one is aware that they are dreaming.

"While I was still sleeping, the whole dream happened as if all at once. I was walking down a dusty trail. To my left and just behind me, I saw a small bird moving about in a bush just atop a hillside. As I drew closer, I walked toward the bush. I reached my hand in and slowly pulled out (what I thought was going to be a bird) a very small, tiny fairy. As I held her in the palm of my hand, I felt enraptured by her. She, baffled and disoriented, came to. So, I asked her, "What is going on here?" She replied, "Well, I think people are getting smaller." Then, all at once, I felt an upward gust behind me. A school of one hundred or so tiny, yellow birds flew out from behind me. At the same time (in real time) I catapulted to my feet and back into reality, I awoke."

Because the dreamer was going to attend a nature walk and discover new things, the fairy could represent impressions which are original. The fairy could also symbolize something related to her feelings about magic and abundance. Not only did the dreamer see a fairy, but birds were also important symbols in the dream. Many symbols were discovered and addressed which helped the dreamer to come to an understanding of its meaning.

Fairy Godmother: The fairy godmother may represent a symbol of what a child wishes their mother would be, with possibilities of being wise, good, magically powerful, and generous.

Giants: Dreaming of a giant may indicate emotions in the child of feeling helpless from being in a world of powerful adults who seem large and capable. The giant can also represent great internal struggles caused by primal forces the child is learning to deal with. The dream giant could appear as a gentle guardian, represented in the story "Aladdin" as a big helpful servant.

Gnomes and dwarfs: Often referred to as the "guardians of the woodlands," the dwarf may symbolize a protector with mischievous childlike behavior. The Gnome often symbolizes peace, playfulness, and happiness.

Jesus: Depending on culture and religious background, asking the child what this symbol represents and what they have been taught about this image is very important when doing a dream interpretation.

Magician: A wicked magician may symbolize deception or the use of knowledge and skills to selfishly satisfy the child's own whims. A good magician may represent appeal, make believe, or pleasant acts of surprise. Magician's generally symbolize the mysterious and powerful, either helpful or harmful.

Witches: Witches may represent the behavior of the child where they are using their intuition and feelings to their own gain. The witch, when appearing as a woman, may symbolize a negative mother image. With the emergence of modern-day fairy-tales portraying the female witch as a beautiful magical creature, a change in beliefs toward the witch has happened. Remember, it is important to consult the child to discover what the witch means to them.

Zombies: Zombies may represent feelings of emptiness, void of emotions, feeling threatened or disconnected, even the fear of death.

A Birth Memory and Recurring Dream

Recurring traumatic dreams can manifest because of unresolved or misunderstood events that may have happened early on in life, even in the womb before birth. David Chamberlain, a California psychologist, author and editor, is a leading authority on birth psychology. He uses hypnotherapy to discover and help resolve traumas that have happened in the womb and at birth. Chamberlain claims that many people from age two and up remember their own beginning. An example of the birth memory experience was told to me one quiet afternoon by my oldest daughter who at the time was four years old. She began by saying, "When I was a little girl I was covered with blood. It was blue, it was blood. I wasn't scared."

"What did it sound like?" I asked her.

"Fumbip, fumbip, my heart said."

"Did it hurt?"

"No, well, it hurt my neck and shoulders and back and nose and head."

"Then what happened?"

"Then the blood was off me."

At the time of my daughter's birth I suffered from a gall bladder attack which caused me to go into false labor. For three days I experienced contractions while frequently vomiting bile. Taking nutritional supplements prescribed by my midwife and eating healing alkaline foods, I returned to wellness. Sensing that the gall bladder attack may have put undue strain on my daughter, who was still in the womb, we chose to go to the hospital to hasten her birth.

While writing this book I asked my children to share some of their dreams and memories. It was during a family gathering one night that my oldest daughter remembered a childhood recurring dream that still haunts her as an adult. In the dream she is standing on an extremely high and narrow staircase without railings, with a never-ending drop off on both sides. Terrified and afraid of falling, she can see no way down from her frightening position. A few days after hearing about her recurring dream I remembered an incident at her birth which may explain the dream's recurrence.

Feeling exhausted after healing from the gall bladder attack, then experiencing a difficult labor, it was with much effort that we were able to get my daughter's head to crown. She appeared to be stuck in the birth canal, so the doctor used forceps to assist with her birth which then happened very quickly. It felt like a powerful suction cup had wrenched the baby from my womb. She was swung into the air with such speed that the look on her face revealed intense fright! Even though doctors were nearby to protect her from falling they were not part of her awareness. I imagine she might have felt terrified, afraid of falling with no way down from her frightening position.

Could the feelings of terror and the fear of falling in her staircase dreams be a memory reflection of her birth experience? It is a good possibility that there is a connection. Over the past few years there has been an increase in information concerning feelings and beliefs established before, during and immediately after birth revealing intimate connections among human beings. From Karol Truman's book *Feelings Buried Alive Never Die*, she quotes Sarah Belle Dougherty, Sunrise Magazine, February/March 1990 *Mysteries of Pre-natal Consciousness,* "The fetus can see, hear, experience, taste and, on a primitive level, even learn in utero. . . Most importantly, he can feel—not with an adult's sophistication, but feel nonetheless."

The mind of a child is not young. It is as old as the subconscious instincts which it contains. According to Carl Jung, Swiss psychiatrist and psychotherapist, there is a collective unconscious where memory is shared by individuals with a common ancestry. This sharing can influence actions and behaviors. The mind's task is to encourage development of the child's individuality and shape their life. In their deep instinctual nature, children know this and fight unceasingly to understand life events while maintaining their individuality. This struggle can be detected in children's dreams which could be considered an exploration of their uniqueness. Understanding the child's dreams with empathy and acceptance are vital for healthy psychological development.

Chapter 6

Lights, Camera, Action!

"And they said one to another, Behold the dreamer cometh."
—Genesis 37:19

Every human action can be used in the dream as a symbol. Without action in dreams there would be no plot or story; so every action should be considered as symbolic and the action and emotion should be analyzed. Listed below are just a few of many possible action symbols.

Key Action Dream Symbols

Automobiles: Driving a car in a dream represents the action of feeling in control in life. Riding in a car may represent the dreamer's feelings of being out of control, or perhaps they are a passenger going along for the ride. To interpret correctly, first determine the type of car in the dream and the emotional connection to it. It could be a truck with power and force, or a little Volkswagen bug moseying along a windy path. Pay attention to what is happening in the dream while driving or being driven.

A young woman in her thirties had a dream where she drove her car and parked it in front of her mother's house. While leaving the car running with her purse still inside and the car door open, she ran inside the house, grabbed what she needed and went back outside to get into her car. To her surprise and horror she discovered that her car was gone! Frantically looking for the car, she noticed it going around the back road. Running quickly to the corner to see who was driving so she could report it to the police, she saw an unfamiliar, shadowed, dark figure with stubble on his face. She said, "A scary, evil presence was driving away in my car! I woke up terrified with my heart pounding."

Driving and feeling in control, then having her car stolen and feeling violated with a loss of control, brought about a frantic desire for the dreamer to regain control. Not only did this young woman feel her control was taken from her, she also felt her values had been stolen. This was done by an action or idea presenting itself as darkness and evil.

Feelings of violation and loss can be terrifying. When dreams like this occur, it is important to evaluate what is transpiring in the dreamer's life so they can begin to establish a safe plan of action to regain control. Making personal choices can create feelings of empowerment which may allow the dreamer the ability to create their own reality. Feelings of safety, grounding and empowerment are natural human conditions needed to be in control.

In the Bible, Genesis chapter one verse twenty six, God's counsel is to have dominion over all things of the earth, "And let them have dominion...over everything... that creepeth upon the earth." Dominion is defined as control and mastery. All human beings have been gifted free will and the ability to create. It is the human birthright and responsibility to become personally empowered masters of life. Enjoying a life of good health and happiness, learning how to take responsibility for personal actions and setting boundaries, are all part of the admonition of having dominion.

Pedal Bike: Riding a pedal bike represents control in life, with the dreamer as the force behind the movement. However, unlike an automobile, riding a bike has less protection because of exposure to the elements. I had a dream while writing this book where my husband and I were riding pedal bikes. We stopped at a shopping center to make a purchase. I had forgotten my coat, the weather was turning cold, and I needed to buy something to keep warm. Gathered at the entrance of the shopping center were several bikers talking with concerned expressions. By asking what was going on, we discovered that various bikers in the area had been attacked by mountain lions and wolves. We were encouraged to be careful in our travels. When I woke up, I realized my dream was revealing feelings of vulnerability while sensing possibilities of attack for writing a book about dreams. There may be critics and disbelievers—my personal wolves and mountain lions— that could try to hurt me.

Drinking: A few drinking metaphors would be the elixir of life, life giving fluids, the land flowing with milk and honey, or the milk of human kindness. Ask the dreamer about the type of beverage they were drinking and its personal significance. When analyzing a dream, refer to the dreamer's meaning of the experience and their feelings towards this process in the dream.

Eating: To most people eating stands for survival or sustenance and possibly prosperity. Whenever the dream of eating presents a satisfied feeling, the connotation would be just that. Sometimes there is specific meaning concerning the type of food being eaten. Remember to ask the dreamer if there is importance concerning the food in the dream.

To dream of feeding people and finding satisfaction would signify the ability to provide mental and spiritual food which is satisfying the part of the dream that the friends would represent. Usually the act of eating typifies the process of incorporating the material taken into the total thought structure of the individual, referred to as "food for thought."

Internal sensations exist while sleeping and can often influence subconscious action in dreams. Sleep makes the dreamer retire into the subconscious and often physical sensations are taken within the psyche upon retiring. Sensations such as hunger can bring about dreams provoked by specific body organs or systems, as in the case with the fasting man. A man in his mid-twenties decided to see how long he could fast (eating nothing and drinking only water). During the seventh night, he had a dream about making and eating a pizza covered with crispy broiled shrimp. He took this dream as a signal that it might be time to end his fast. The food dreams stopped with the conclusion of his fast, but the "curiosity about what a shrimp pizza might taste like," persisted!

Eliminating: The action symbols in these dreams usually describe the ways the dreamer is trying to eliminate old hurts, fears, guilt, or anything that may clog the emotional system. An example would be where the dreamer cannot eliminate because of dirty toilets. Perhaps they feel that it would be dirty and nasty to express their personal concerns and troubles.

There are also dreams of eliminating that may be connected to the need for creativity or a desire to release imaginative abilities. The dreamer feels unable to experience release because of a lack of privacy, or the difficulty in finding the proper place to do the elimination.

Riding on animals: Ask for the dreamer's associations with the particular animal and go from there. For example, riding on oxen could signify a primitive or slow going way of living.

Running: Running may have different representations depending on the setting in the dream and the type of running. Some forms of running can symbolize a running away from problems, a feeling or need to escape from danger, exercise and exhilaration, festivity, or the feeling of always being on the go or trying to keep up with the demands of life.

A middle aged woman dreamed about a male friend who was a quadriplegic. In this dream she noticed that the two of them were going to a church meeting. The man was thinner and healthier than in real life with a butch hair style which gave him a clean-cut appearance. The woman's friend was so happy that he ran ahead of her as they entered the building to go to their meeting. The woman realized that he was using some type of mechanical device to assist him with running. She was thrilled with his freedom and abilities. When her friend reached the door of the building, he looked back at her with a broad smile emanating deep happiness!

The dreamer revealed that she was at a time in her life where she was experiencing a sense of sacredness and value. This place of value was represented in the dream by a church. Her friend symbolized a crippled action and idea that was now free to go fast and experience joy. Through a mechanical device, which the dreamer said represented her computer, she was able to accomplish and create more things than she could have ever imagined. She felt there was so much for her to do that she could barely keep up with all her ideas and goals.

The running of her friend and his joyful happy face symbolized her feelings about the ideas and projects she was working on. Those actions and ideas were invigorating, clean and precise or focused, which were presented in the dream by the friend's butch haircut. The activities of growth and learning that she was enjoying were good for her, symbolized in the dream by the healthier look of her friend.

By understanding the dream message, the woman experienced a sense of freedom that allowed her to continue on her path of exploration. She felt that she was given permission to continue in her valuable personal search and that she could do so with joy and happiness!

Sexual Intercourse: This is a very common symbol which appears in dreams sometimes causing distress to the dreamer because of the violation of conscious moral codes. The sexual union often symbolizes the creative act, the conception of a new life, and may also signify the union of a new aspect of the dreamer's personality. The act of uniting with another person is symbolic of connecting with an action or idea, feeling or emotion that the dreamer is considering incorporating into life.

When intercourse is presented as rape, it often represents the violation and intrusion of privacy. Some dreams portray the fear of rape with no actual action of rape taking place. The dreamer must identify what the rapist represents to them and address that association. For example, the fear of being raped by a large and aggressive man (a male figure often symbolizes actions and ideas in dreams) may represent the actions of aggression the dreamer is internally experiencing. These actions could include compelling forms of sensuality, extreme appetites, greed or other bodily functions.

To accurately interpret sexual dreams, it is important to get the associations that go with the characters and actions involved. Extreme caution should be used when interpreting sexual dream symbols as these types of dreams are often filled with guilt. For example, when a boy first experiences night emissions, it can be as disturbing as a young girl who begins menstruation. No matter what the age of the dreamer, because of the personal emotional nature of the dream, they must be ready and willing to understand the messages that these types of dreams are revealing.

Storms: There are many types of storms that can be experienced in dreams such as thunderstorms, hurricanes, hailstorms, or even sand storms. Each dreamer will have a personal perspective on the meaning of the storm, whether it is symbolic of "emotional turmoil", or "stormy thoughts", with a representation of conflict between the mind and the heart. People often connect words such as struggle, misfortune, shock, fear and loss to stormy situations and conflicts in life.

While writing this book I had a dream that portrayed some of the daily fears I was experiencing. It began with myself, along with neighboring friends and family, at an outside community function. While visiting with a friend, I happened to look over toward the horizon and saw a tornado coming. The tornado was horrifying. After warning everybody at the function, we scattered running for safety.

In my fear and hurry to find a place of refuge until the tornado passed, I lost my phone which was my mode of communication with my children. It was while hunting for safety that I saw an unfamiliar, scared, little girl. I thought she probably lived at a nearby house. Together we rushed to find cover and went down some stairs to the left of a large house, underneath a gray cement overhang by the stairs. We watched with panic as the powerful tornado came directly toward us. It struck a gas station with massive force which caused a devastating explosion. An enormous black-orange fiery ball came toward us and we shivered with fear as it roared past. The ball of fire moved so quickly that we were not affected by it at all; however, it did cause monumental destruction along with the tornado.

After the storm passed I tried to find my children, but couldn't because I didn't have my phone. Then the scene changed and I found myself driving with my husband down the road. We went through some gentle rolling hills where we found dead mangled snakes scattered all over the road. Some snakes were gigantic with glimmering scales, a few were normal in size and others were small, looking much like garden snakes. The scene changed again and I found myself in a place of safety, in someone else's house, with my mom and children. Their father had come over and given us a video to watch. I remember feeling excited because I thought, "Oh, that's a fun video. Watch something happy."

Upon awakening I thought how strange that dream was. Dreams can seem so unrelated and fractured. Looking closer at the dream I discovered a profound message. Reviewing my activities during the days preceding the dream I remembered that I had been listening to and watching shows that were destructive (the tornado), poisoning my thoughts (the snakes were the poison), and creating fear. My faith was lost (my phone), which caused me to lose my connection to the actions and ideas, feelings and emotions (my children), that were most dear to me. My mother was a constant presence throughout the dream. She represented my closest feelings and strong foundation of emotions related to faith, joy and love. The dream message was a reminder of how vital it is to watch and listen to uplifting and inspiring messages which build faith and trust, not fear and doubt.

Swimming: Swimming dreams often symbolize attempts at dealing with emotions and life situations. An example of a swimming dream was shared with me by a man in his late fifties. His dream began at a public swimming pool where he was having fun swimming. As he was happily swimming, he noticed that the pool was only a few feet deep with water. All the swimmers were busy swimming, appearing to have fun, including him. Then he realized that he was swimming without any water. He was still having fun, but was scraping his belly on the bottom of the pool. When he got out of the pool he recognized what was happening and decided that he no longer wanted to swim without water while scraping the bottom of the pool with his body, even if he could do so while making the experience enjoyable.

This dream came at a time when the man had been struggling to find employment that he enjoyed. He had some money in savings and had experimented with several entrepreneurial opportunities, but he did not find anything that brought in enough money. Even though he was having fun pursuing these new ventures, he realized he was tired of financially scraping by. Once he understood the meaning of the dream his desire for employment which would produce reliable income increased. He found a job that provided enough money for a comfortable life which was pleasurable as well.

Trains: There are trains of thought and trains of action and emotion, all engineered with purpose. Trains may represent a powerful transport guided by a predetermined direction.

An explosive train dream was told to me by a young mother. This dream was very disturbing to her and caused much confusion. After the dream she woke up feeling disoriented and sad. By helping her understand the dream's message, she felt comfort and grew in awareness concerning what her sub-conscious was revealing regarding emotions about her current life situation.

The dream began with her sister-in-law and sister-in-law's husband getting married. In reality they were married, but in the dream they had been together for a long time, had all three of their daughters and had never gotten married. They chose to get married on a moving train with their wedding party utilizing three large passenger cars. In the dreamer's words, "My mother and father-in-law were there, several other in-laws were present, although some spouses were missing. My children were there, but my husband was not. My parents, many of my cousins, aunts and uncles were also in attendance. It was interesting that my relatives were there even though they were completely unrelated to the couple getting married.

As we were all gathered and the train was rolling along, the train started to shake and a strange man, someone I had never seen before, a person who looked like my husband but was not, ran through the train telling everyone that they needed to gather their things and jump off the train before it exploded! Everyone scrambled to their living quarters to grab anything they could, including luggage, coats, hats and scarves. I picked up three different coats, put on a blue hat, grabbed my purse and headed toward a group of children to help them get ready. I started to panic because I didn't know where my own children were; there were adults everywhere, so I prayed over and over that someone would take care of them.

My sister-in-law and I prepared the children to jump off the train by opening the doors. Outside the train there was a twenty foot drop into a few feet of snow. The train was on a bridge that appeared to have no end. My sister-in-law jumped first, I sent the children out one by one, then I jumped. When I stood up I was relieved to see that no one was harmed, but all the belongings were scattered everywhere and we were all freezing.

My mom and Aunt appeared with our group, along with two of my daughters and one of my nieces. Then my cousin, who is not a very good person in reality (liar, cheater, thief, manipulator), showed up with a bag around his neck. I ignored him because I had so much on my mind. I was panicking because I couldn't find my baby, we were lost and we didn't know what to do next. Even though I was surrounded by family, I felt very alone. While in this confused state of panic, my cousin walked up to me and handed me the bag. I looked inside and there was my baby! She was bundled and warm, completely unharmed. I burst into tears and thanked him for saving my daughter while I put the bag over my shoulder.

We decided to prepare to move and find safety. With all the children on my husband's side of the family, and some of my cousin's children, we began to bundle everyone up with several outfits to keep as warm as possible. I took a bottle of essential oil from my purse, I never left home without it, and passed it around for everyone to use to help them stay calm. When it came back to me there was none left. I tossed the bottle aside and started looking for shoes. To my amazement, we all landed by an obscure, out-of-the-way fence that was lined with hundreds of pairs of different sized shoes! The fence went on for miles and didn't seem to lead to anything. Everybody took two pair of shoes, one bigger than the other and put the larger pair over the smaller one to keep their feet warm.

Once all the children were bundled and had extra shoes on, we decided to follow the fence to see if it led to a town, or perhaps someplace where we could call for and receive help. We walked for what seemed like hours. Most of the children were in tears and every adult, plus the older youth, was carrying smaller children. My sister-in-law noticed a cloud of smoke off in the distance. Hoping it was the train and maybe more people, we walked toward it as fast as we could. We discovered it was a section of the train that had exploded. Keeping the children huddled outside the compartment near some of the burning debris to get warm, I went inside to make sure it was safe before allowing the others to enter. If it was safe, they could come inside to warm up before we continued on our journey.

As I entered the train I noticed that it was put together in an unusual manner. There were compartments spaced in different lengths, some a foot wide and others only an inch wide, but the total length of the section of train was normal size. Injured people I didn't recognize were everywhere. One person I did recognize was a friend of mine, a good family friend since childhood. I asked her if she had seen anyone else in the family. We were so close as friends that we considered each other to be family. She told me that before this part of the train fell off, my pregnant cousin, her husband and two children had died in the explosion. I was devastated!

I knelt down and cried for the longest time. Then my

friend told me that before the explosion, she had seen my brother-in-law, my dad, father-in-law and the strange man who gave the warning about the explosion. That was before we all jumped and before her part of the train exploded then fell off the bridge. She didn't remember anything after that. Her husband, an EMT, was bleeding internally and wasn't going to live much longer. She told me not to worry about them, but to get the children to safety. I put on a brave face and went back outside. My mother-in-law was there with a broken leg, as well as my cousin who had a big gash on her head. She had no idea where her little boy was. We were all in a panic! That is when I woke up feeling very disoriented and sad."

I talked with the dreamer about daily events during the time of the dream and learned that some recent situations she had experienced left her feeling emotionally distraught. These events changed her belief system about life, marriage and motherhood. The death of relatives in the dream represents the loss of feelings and emotions, actions and ideas that she had once closely related with. Her new life situation brought about a death of those beliefs she once cherished.

Her subconscious was revealing feelings that the journey she began in life should have been a celebration, a happy union. However, the train, a powerful force on a predetermined direction symbolizing her expectations about life, was thrown off track by a series of powerful life changing events. The shoes in her dream, a soul language message that she has been given a lot of comfort and support on her journey, brought her peace. She said, "The shoes represent family support and comfort I have experienced, things I am very grateful for." Because of the dream message reminding her of family support, and her determination to be courageous, "put on a brave face," she has hope of survival, even with the difficult journey ahead.

Walking: Dreams of walking may represent the use of natural abilities, a way that one travels through life. Dreaming of being in a vehicle traveling, then walking may symbolize the dreamers desire to discover their natural means before they can succeed or reach their destination. Walking alone may represent independence, while walking with another person may indicate a willingness to identify with others.

Wearing shoes: Feet represent the base with which the body stands and may stand for attitudes in life or positions taken. Shoes usually show ways in which the dreamer dresses their understanding. If the shoes being worn stand out in the dream, pay attention to their appearance. If they are new, they could represent beneficial changes. If they are old and worn, they may symbolize humility or servitude. Ask the dreamer how they feel about the shoes that have been brought into focus during the dream.

Dreams and emotions are like visiting new, out of the ordinary places, full of key words and symbols. In the beginning there may be knowledge of only a few key words and symbols. The more symbols that are learned, the more meaning and awareness there will be toward the messages in dreams. With continued learning the soul language will grow and there will be success and greater understanding to messages revealed in dreams.

Chapter 7

Of the Kingdom Animalia

"The girl dreams she is dangerously ill. Suddenly birds come out of her skin and cover her completely...Swarms of gnats obscure the sun, the moon, and all the stars except one. That one star falls upon the dreamer."
—C.G. Jung, Man and His Symbols

There is a large group of feelings that are related to the animal instincts which are symbolized by various animals. Humankind has been using animals as a symbolic bridge between instinctual emotions and expressive words describing emotions for a long time.

Animal Symbols

Bull: Hearing the word "bull" often brings images of non-castrated male bovine animals used for breeding. Terms like "bull headed" and "the bull in a china shop" are used when describing certain personalities. Bulls are seen as aggressive, powerful animals, physically strong and muscular with a masculine identity. In comparison, oxen would be considered dull, plodding, or resigned which could symbolically represent the loss of creativity. Depending on the person's association with the bull, it could signify a variety of things. To a farmer it may represent fertility, to a bullfighter, sport, and to other people, a danger of attack.

Cat: Throughout history cats have been referred to as guardians of the underworld, stoic, silent and mysterious. To some there is a strong association of witchcraft with dark psychic intuitive functions. They frequently display an attitude of being haughty and aloof. To a few they may represent a sense of the sadistic ones because of their instincts for ferreting out mice, rats and other unwanted creatures. Cat lovers think of them as playful and cuddly. They sometimes represent a harmless vulnerability with flair toward the feminine side.

The feline cat fights ferociously to protect her young. She may also symbolize feminine selfishness, fighting underhandedly and ruthlessly while competing with other females.

The Tom cat prowls in the dark for sex and food, alone, sensate, with a feline grace, a gigolo. He refuses the masculine value of team work and cooperation while enjoying the isolation.

The wild cats such as the panthers, leopards, jaguars, or tigers, live in a wild state of ruthlessness, treachery, howling and scratching, ready to pounce upon their prey at any time.

Cow: Because of milk that the cow furnishes, she is often referred to as a maternal figure and in some societies she is looked upon as the sacred figure of mother goddess. She is a docile creature who chews her cud which can represent rehashing what she takes in. As she is often found grazing, unaware of her surroundings but strong in her position, she has the ability of endurance while she turns vegetation into milk, a form of giving, reproducing and nourishing without knowing.

Dog: A dog symbol has many meanings. It can stand for a type of fierce attacking animal instinct or it can represent wild instincts that have been tamed. The dog may symbolize a loyal faithful nature of fidelity and friendship.

There are different types of dogs such as lap dogs who bring feelings of being loved and babied without too much responsibility, show dogs who cater to man's pride and need for attention, bulldogs who represent tenacity and determination, blood hounds which tackle the culprits, or hounds of hell which can represent guilt and shame. Police dogs are guardians; shepherd dogs are protectors and the St. Bernard, rescuers that search for and save man from cold and dangerous places.

Birds: Birds often symbolize freedom, life and messengers of deity. Whereas the eagle, known as skilled hunters and the King of the birds, is the ruler of the sky connected to the elements with a strong mental awareness. Eagles often represent authority, sovereignty, leadership and fearlessness.

A dream featuring a predatory bird of prey was told to

me by a young mother who recently married. In her dream she found herself climbing to the top of a pine tree with her adolescent daughter. Her daughter appeared older in the dream than she was in real life. The daughter was climbing the tree to investigate an eagle's nest. "Be careful," the mother told her, "Eagles are predators!" The eagle took a wary look at the daughter, but didn't hurt her. The daughter knew she wouldn't be hurt because she had been there before, so it was no big deal for her to be there again. When the mother realized that the eagle was there to protect her young and was not a danger, she began to recognize that their position up in the tree was the real threat.

As the daughter began to climb down from the top of the tree, she fell and broke her arm; however, the mother was softly lowered to the ground by the tree with a gentle bowing motion. After being lowered to the ground, the mother noticed some boys on bikes and asked them to help carry her daughter home.

When they arrived home the mother found a man at the house who looked like her father. At second glance she realized he was someone familiar, but not related. The mother began to tell the man that she needed to get her daughter to the emergency room. While the mother was driving to the emergency room with her daughter in the front seat and the man in the back seat, the man told her that she took the daughter to the emergency room a lot and was overprotective of her. At hearing this she felt that the man was chastising her. Then the mother yelled at the man and said, "She fell down forty feet and broke her arm!" She was so mad that she threw a protein bar at him while telling him how much she hated him.

Knowledge and understanding of the symbols being represented by the dreamer are necessary in the beginning analysis of the dream. To make this process easier to understand, I have placed the dreamer's symbolic meanings in parenthesis:

A young mother found herself climbing to the top of a pine tree (a peaceful and serene place) with her adolescent daughter (young, closely related feelings and emotions to be protected). Her daughter appeared older in the dream than she was in real life (the dreamer feels more independent than she realizes). The daughter began to climb (reach a different level) the tree to investigate an eagle's nest (a place of protection, a home, a family). "Be careful," the mother told her, "Eagles are predators!" The eagle (predator or danger) took a wary look at the daughter, but didn't hurt her. The daughter (the dreamer's closely related feelings and emotions) knew she wouldn't be hurt because she had been there before (the dreamer had this emotional connection before and felt safe in this place), so it was no big deal for her to be there again. When the mother realized that the eagles were not a danger, she began to feel that their position (her situation in life) up in the tree was the real threat.

As the daughter began to climb down (this represents a change in the level of her feelings and emotions) from the top of the tree, she fell and broke her arm (a broken ability to function); however, the mother was softly lowered to the ground by the tree with a gentle bowing motion (the mother felt that she was being guided). There were some boys (young unrelated actions and ideas) on bikes that helped carry the daughter home (a place of protection and comfort, a structure of her beliefs). When they arrived home the mother found a man at the house who looked like her father (familiar actions and ideas of authority). At second glance she realized he was someone familiar but not related.

The mother began to tell the man that she needed to get her daughter to the emergency room (a place to receive immediate help). While the mother was driving (she is in charge of her path) to the emergency room with her daughter in the front seat and the man in the back seat, the man told her that she took the daughter to the emergency room (needed immediate help) a lot and was overprotective (sheltered) of her. At hearing this she felt that the man was chastising (punishing) her. Then the mother yelled at the man and said, "She fell down forty feet and broke her arm!" She was so mad that she threw a protein bar (energy) at him while telling him how much she hated him (hated the ideas and actions the man represented).

By finding and defining the symbols of the dream, the dreamer's beliefs about family, its function and protection were revealed. The eagle, a key symbol in the dream, represented leadership, fearlessness, and protection which were appealing to the dreamer, for she had visited this place or these feelings in her life before. When in the dream, the dreamer didn't relate to the man whom she believed should symbolize the familiar action and idea of the leader in the home. He did not fit her belief system of how a family leader should function. This resulted in feelings of being punished instead of being helped by the man who should be her fearless protector, her leader. She hated the action and idea that this familiar figure represented because it was not like her related actions and ideas of what a family or father figure should correspond to. The dreamer used her angry energy against these actions and ideas while she was trying to get to a place of healing.

When two families become joined through marriage, as was the case with this young woman, there is often an adjustment period where dissimilar action and ideas need to merge as one to create a healthy family unit. This process can be difficult and frustrating, full of emotional pain at many different levels. At the time of the dream this young mother was going through an adjustment cycle in her new marriage. After analyzing the dream, she realized why she was hurting emotionally, saw the source of her anger and knew that it was up to her to seek help and fix what felt like a broken ability to function. Eventually she found ways to understand and cope with her new life situation and began to change her beliefs about how her marriage should be, to possibilities of what it could become.

Elephant: Considered the largest animal on earth, the elephant is often associated with wisdom, a long memory, caution, great strength, prosperity, good luck, and power. They seem to possess a sixth sense concerning possible danger. Elephants are loyal and capable of love, but revengeful to those who may hurt or annoy them. In dreams they often represent the unchanging part of man's instinctual nature.

Goat: These animals are very independent because they can sustain themselves in situations where other animals would generally starve. They have been associated with attitudes of belligerence, hardheadedness, and stubbornness. Seen as curious creatures with a determined nature, goats are sometimes viewed as symbols who "rush headlong" into situations unable to see where they are going. They may also represent an attitude of solidarity with an air of high spiritual ambitions.

A "scapegoat" is a metaphor for one that bears the blame of others. The term originated from a later translation in the writings of the Bible, specifically Leviticus 16:8 "And Aaron shall cast lots upon the two goats; one lot for the Lord, and the other lot for the scapegoat."

A Billy Goat is a breeder. We sometimes refer to a certain type of old man abnormally preoccupied with sex as an "old goat," as dangerous and troublesome as an angry and marauding old goat would be.

Horse: The horse has carried man's burdens, plowed fields, supported men in battle and brought enjoyment to man through horse races and shows. They represent a noble beast with power, grace, beauty, vitality and strength. When appearing in color during dreams they might represent a variety of things. A brown horse may symbolize earthly forces, where black or white horses typify the energy of darkness or light. They may embody and symbolize the life force of an individual.

As a Reiki Master Teacher, I have occasionally had the honor of sensing what I call a person's soul essence. This "soul essence" is a type of energy stream or dominant life force that usually reveals itself in the form of a symbol, much like those found in dreams. Over the past few years I have been shown the essence of several people, two of whom were women with the symbol of the horse.

When this soul message is revealed, emblematic words follow. These words describe the meaning of the symbol bringing out light and shadow sides which belong to the essence. When the person is in the light side of the symbol, there is balance and contentment in their life. When they are living the shadow side, there is often discomfort and sometimes illness. One woman's horse appeared as a highly spirited black stallion boasting a lengthy wavelike mane. The other woman's essence appeared as a strong and muscular chocolate brown work horse, generating an inner calm and a deep unending display of strength.

When I told each person of their "soul essence" each one confirmed its accuracy and shared feelings about what their symbol represented to them. This process is similar to that of the dream symbols and their meanings. No two people have the same essence meaning, and no two dreamers often have identical meanings for their dream symbols.

Lion: The lion, king and most invulnerable of beasts, represents the life of a great fighter who stands for self-respect, intelligence, freedom and royalty! He symbolizes instinctual courage and wisdom as a protector and an admirable father. In history there are stories of Richard the Lionhearted, a man of great courage, strength and endurance, who symbolizes the image of the mighty king!

The Bible mentions that the lion will be among many animals that shall lie down with the lamb when man comes into true understanding. All the characteristics of the lion can be developed and expressed by any individual. One aspect of maturity is the combining of the gentleness and humility of the lamb with the strength and courage of the lion.

Mouse: The mouse typifies a small annoyance, great timidity and lack of courage. They generally represent a type of disease carrier and petty thief. This pettiness may symbolize the taking of small trivial satisfactions which one does not have a right to. The mouse may signify the knowing of getting out of places or how to get into them by using little persistent effort. A mouse could also correspond to a method of analyzing by taking small pieces of a situation to find a way out of difficulty rather than forcing a way out.

Pig: Pigs have been associated with the grosser side of human behavior for years, even though they are clean and represent fertility and honesty in many other cultures. Pigs are often associated with greediness, filth, stubbornness and gullibility. The pigs fattened for slaughter are often thought of as stupid, lacking loyalty and love.

Rat: Symbolizing complete self-seeking with no scruples, they are carriers of pestilence and plague, thriving on dead bodies. They could possibly represent a scavenger, greed, a vindictive type of personality and maybe even selfishness. However, to some, they make great pets and show intelligence and industry. In discussing dream symbols with a friend of mine, he reminded me of the Chinese Zodiac and what the rat symbolizes. It ranks first in the Chinese Zodiac with word representations of spirit, ambition, wit, alertness, flexibility and even charisma. Knowing that there are often different meanings for symbols to each dreamer, remember to ask the dreamer for their meaning of the dream symbols.

Sheep: An animal that is easily led; they submissively follow their shepherd and obey his calls. They are a passive creature symbolizing love, goodness, gentleness and vulnerability.

Snake: Most people see the snake represented as the sly one, the deceiver, the tempter. However, there are various meanings for a variety of different snakes. For example, the rattle snake gives warning, the cobra is a symbol of smothering and unselfish giving clinging to what could be called love, but is actually greed. The little venomous snakes that strike when least expected may represent small out of sight things posing as subtle dangers, poisoning thoughts and actions.

Different colored snakes may carry different meanings. Two examples would be the green snake which is likely to signify an instinctual earthly drive, and the black snake which typically represents black magic. Snakes represent significant things to the dreamer depending on their context and the dreamer's interpretation of the symbols in the dream. The following are two completely different representations of snakes in dreams and their meanings to the dreamers.

A Man's Snake Dream

"I am in a house or school and I notice snakes on the counter. I go along outside and I notice an infestation of snakes. They are everywhere. Snakes can hurt you! The snakes are on the counters and the ground, at least ten of them. These snakes are gold; yellow, with diamond shaped heads, sidewinders. I know they are dangerous because of the shape of their heads. I hunt for a stick, something to use as I deal with them. One is coming after me. 'Where the heck is a stick? Sticks are everywhere when you don't need them!'

Now I am in a yard or field, no grass; the dirt is the same color as the snakes. I see three or four snakes out there. 'Son, get a stick!' My son grabs the snakes by the head and throws them to the ground killing them. Then, I see a broom, and I smack the snakes until I am sure they are dead and no longer dangerous. I get rid of all the snakes, for now. Without the broom stick I am scared of them, with the broom stick I have some fear, but it's mostly gone, because with the stick I can deal with them."

In analyzing this dream, it is important to note that during the time of the dream this man was going through training for a new job. The dream began in a school or house. The dream's school or house represented the building where the man had recently finished his schooling, his new job training. During this training he could see the dangers (the snakes) he would have to face and conquer. The training was difficult for him and at times scary. He said that after he came home from training he was immediately put into the "field" to make his contacts. As he went from door to door, he felt unprepared and unarmed without the proper tools he needed to be successful.

In the dream his son represented a closely related action and idea that the man had about tackling his fears. He knew deep down inside, in his closely related beliefs and ideas, that he needed to grab and attack his fears, but having a tool would make the job a lot less stressful and fearful. Once he understood the dream, he realized that with the proper tool(s) the fear would leave and success would follow. He began focusing his efforts on finding and refining effective tools. After his first week in the field he learned how to handle the "snakes" he was facing and found a tool that made his job feel safer while he attacked and killed his fears.

A Child's Snake Dream

"I had a dream about worms. I saw a worm turn into a frog. I was in school alone except with a kid with three worms. He picked one up and I asked if I could hold the worm. I put it back with its friends. There was a snake that went into the box. One worm got scared, they all turned into frogs. The snake went into the frog, and then the snake was a ghost. Then the snake turned real and wrapped around my neck and slept. It didn't kill me."

I asked the child to tell me what worms are. She said, "They are like caterpillars, but without feet, they eat dirt. Some worms I don't like." Then I asked her to tell me about frogs. She said, "They hop and rib-bit. Some frogs are poisonous; I don't like frogs because they are poisonous. Frogs jump on you!" As we continued the discussion, I asked her about snakes. "They slither sideways. I like snakes because I like fierce animals. I like tigers and lions and bears. My dream was cool, worms into frogs!"

As an interpreter it is important to keep personal meanings of the symbols out of the dream analysis. Ask the dreamer what those representations mean to them. Animal instincts in dreams are given to serve as a protective, lifesaving wisdom needed to help satisfy physical needs until enough intelligence is gained to take over the job of conscious self-direction.

As in the dream with the child, a person who has not learned to direct their instincts is still immature. Young children's dreams are simple and naïve and the symbols in them are usually apparent, for children are not afraid to say what they mean. Their experiences are not extensive and they are still in a position of almost complete dependency upon parents. Because young children are vague in their identification with self, their emotions are ruled to an extent by instincts that are animalistic in nature. Their ideas and inspirations are often projected as imaginary creatures such as worms turning into frogs, ghost snakes, fairies and angels or even perhaps witches.

Spider: The spider is a creative symbol, one which weaves the patterns in life and death. She is a skilled, tenacious and resourceful representation of a wise and sometimes deadly teacher. In some cultures she is seen as invincible and in other areas she is viewed as a creator goddess. To others she represents an important part of the animal kingdom and in some societies she is a legend.

A teenager had a disturbing spider dream. In his dream he had let the dog out to go potty, but when he called her to come back in the house he saw large, hairy, spider looking creatures crawling among the weeds. He noticed the dog by the fence where there were more large hairy spiders. He kept calling for the dog who finally moseyed on over to the door, unaware and unconcerned with the dangers around her. When he opened the door to let the dog in, a giant spider came running up behind her. The dog made it inside, but the spider's head caught in the door. The young man said he fell and the creature extended its carnivorous mouth as it tried to bite him in the leg.

In talking with the boy about his dream, he told me that he was very scared of spiders, especially ones that were going to hurt him or come into his house. If we look at the spiders as symbols of something deadly, his house as a place of dwelling for his feelings of security and the dog representing friendship and loyalty, then we can see a message in the dream. At first the young man was not even aware of the dangers to his feelings of friendship and loyalty which could threaten his security. Then his attention was drawn to the dangers lurking around, stalking, ready to attack at any time. Still not too concerned, but aware, he opened the door to his feelings of friendship and loyalty which brought them in to a place of protection, but he slipped which permitted life threatening dangers access into his protected place. By slipping he felt threatened and at risk. The dream was telling him that his security dealing with friendship and loyalty had been threatened because of something he may have done and it was a dangerous and scary thing for him to experience.

Later in another dream he found himself at a youth church activity with a box of large spiders. In the box there was an ordinary tarantula, a spider from the movie "Vampire's Assistant," and a third spider which was a large black widow. The boy placed the box of spiders on the kitchen counter only for a moment. He said, "Some idiot knocked it over and the large arachnids escaped!" Attempting over and over to acquire the creatures, he began to grab them by their backs. Then he tried to grab them with kitchen tongs without success, but finally he left them to wander while he kept an eye on the worst one, the large black widow.

After the dream he mentioned that he somewhat conquered his fear of spiders. "I don't mind them as much, only when they invade my space. Usually I just let them be." The young man realized that the dangers that invaded his sacred places of security were no longer a threat to him. He chose to "let them be" which removed the threat they once represented. In his own interpretation and through his own realization he has shown a type of maturity that comes with growth and awareness.

Wolf: To the pioneers who experienced starvation and drought, the appearance of the wolf meant the threat of starvation. To the Romans, known as mighty warriors, the wolf represented fierceness in their sons. There is an ancient myth about Romulus and Remus who were twin brothers abandoned by their parents as babies and raised by a female wolf. The wolf nursed the babies for a while until they were found by a shepherd who raised them. When the twins reached adulthood they decided to establish a city where the wolf had discovered them. In quarreling over where the site should be, Remus was killed by his brother. This left Romulus as the sole founder of the new city which he named Rome. The allegory of Romulus and Remus is much like a dream. As twin brothers nurtured by a wolf, they were nursed in her fierceness through her milk.

There are several individual meanings of the wolf depending on a person's association with the creature.

Someone who lives on the edge of a forest would perceive a wolf differently than someone who has only ever seen a wolf in a zoo. A person who has lived in poverty and has a deep instinctual desire for survival or a need to satisfy their hunger may perceive a wolf in a dream as someone dangerously preying upon values in a ruthless way. Wolves can be seen as deceptive, dangerous, evil, wild, strong, animalistic, mystical, protectors, guardians, loyal, communicators, intelligent, cunning, predatory, vicious, or even admirable, depending on the dreamer's personal experiences and beliefs.

To some people, symbolism is a form representing beauty, while others believe symbols and their functions are to serve as objects that are merely nonfunctional. Others may think that there is no such thing as symbolism, that a wolf is just a wolf. In some cases that may be true. For the dreamer who wishes to know and understand meaning in dreams, keep an open mind to possible symbols revealed in dreams. Embrace the idea that dreams may be a way of revealing answers for a life that was meant to be enjoyed.

Chapter 8

The Human Factor

"Standing on the bare ground,—my head bathed by the
blithe air and uplifted into infinite space,—
all mean egotism vanishes.
I become a transparent eyeball; I am nothing; I see all;
the currents of the Universal Being circulate through me;
I am part or parcel of God."
—Ralph Waldo Emerson

*P*eople in dreams often symbolize human feelings. For example, if a woman is struggling with the desire to gossip, she may dream of females among her associations that are known as people who gossip. When men struggle with feelings for control, similar to that of a dictator, they may dream of someone who has a corresponding dictatorship type personality.

Women have difficulties thinking of themselves as men in dreams so they associate themselves more with women and men have a tendency to associate themselves more with men. A man in a woman's dream may symbolize her own actions, ideas or logical processes, since men are associated with actions, logic and ideas in the conscious world. A woman appearing in a man's dream is likely to symbolize his intuition, love, tenderness, softness or any of the emotions in which he associates with women.

Men's Dream Symbols

A Man's Father, Brother, Son, Grandfather and Grandson: A man relates his actions and ideas according to male patterns and activities he has experienced in life. *Father* is the image of masculinity patterns which a man will strive to achieve or avoid. *Brother* may represent accepted values most like his own. A man's *son* may represent possible projections of himself or a continuation of self. The *Grandfather* may represent ancient family laws, physical heritage and traditions. A *grandson* may symbolize actions and ideas toward hope and wishes for the future. Each action pattern would have some special meaning or trait, whether feared or loved, for the dreamer.

A Man's Mother, Grandmother, Sister, Wife, Daughter, Granddaughter: Men generally focus on actions, productivity and ideas, leaving the feelings and emotions which build relationships to the women in their lives. Women who express and represent these emotions are generally women they know and associate with. Usually the first woman in his life, the *mother,* contributes to feelings and intuition, moral and spiritual standards, good and evil.

She may provide the emotional food that nourishes and sustains his actions and ideas. A *grandmother* may symbolize wisdom and security or comfort during times of trial. The *sister* may represent closely related feelings, emotions and intuitions which come through heredity and environment.

A man's *wife*, his emotional companion and help meet, is the man's choice of emotional habits, the great body of feelings, emotions and intuitions that he has chosen to build his life around, which embodies the picture of his own emotional worth. As the mother of his children, the man's wife often represents his hopes of the future and the promise of what tomorrow will bring through his seed.

A man's *daughter* may symbolize his hopes concerning his emotional future. *Granddaughters* represent a man's feelings and emotions that may have been kept in the background while he faced the world of work and ambition. She may represent acceptance of his soft and tender emotions, which if accepted, can symbolize the harvest of his life and heredity. Remember, each symbol often has a specific meaning, so ask the dreamer what the female in the dream my represent.

Romanticized Feminine Representations: Eve, Harlot, Virgin, Muse, Goddess: To a man, each woman in his life will characterize certain modified roles in his dreams, ideals, daydreams and imagined emotional experiences. *Eve,* portrayed as the mother of all living, may represent a temptress knowing "good from evil" or a companion and help meet. Sometimes seen as the rib of man, the intuition part of man, the part that helps him feel complete, she may also symbolize the man's temptation and compulsion to plant his seed and perpetuate himself upon the earth. As the mother of all living she may also represent Mother Nature with her instinctual necessity to reproduce and sustain life.

The *Harlot* may represent free and unethical uses of sex, threat of disease and disgrace or whatever the man's feelings are about his self worth. A man brought up formally who later learns different sex standards, may imagine a woman as both virgin and harlot. He may want to marry and live with the virgin image, but be attracted and stimulated by only the harlot. A man may dream of his mother as a harlot when he feels he is being exploited by her. The mother's deep love and desire to hold onto him by using seductive techniques may make him feel exploited. When the mother has not found satisfaction in her own marriage, she tries to compensate by building a relationship with her son. Too much caressing, too much woman to man emotion in a mother son relationship is unhealthy for both of them. This type of overprotection and over direction can rob the young man of his chance to mature.

A *virgin* often has deep religious significance. She may represent the best side in the man, his spiritual nature and awareness of his creator which inspires him to be unselfish in his manhood. The virgin image may also represent a picture of sterile virginity symbolizing the inability to be giving, which may bring about difficulties in blending and may cause problems in attaining happiness in sexually intimate relationships.

The *muse* is the motivating figure of understanding and knowledge that can bring inspiration and belief for dreams to come true. She may symbolize the fire of man's creativity, the power that makes him desire to produce great works of art and accomplish magnificent deeds! She can spring from his growing emotional nature which is beneath the level of conscious awareness giving her the capacity to be a beneficial influence. While the muse may inspire, dreaming of a *goddess* may be overemphasizing emotion, intuition and spiritual values. He may be sacrificing his natural ideas and instincts, as well as spiritual values. He may feel emotionally castrated similar to the castration in ancient times when a man took an oath to serve such visionary goddesses.

Dream Example: A Man's Mother Dream

A friend of mine told me a dream that began with he and his mother at her home. Her place was located in an area known for positive energy and vortexes. She suggested that they go meditate at a vortex, but he was hesitant to go. He mentioned that he had turned her offer down to meditate too many times, so reluctantly he said, "Yes, let's go and do it." The next thing he knew, they were sitting in a medicine wheel meditating. As he sat there he thought, "I don't see what the big deal is about this," when all of a sudden everything got really bright! He remembered thinking that they must have traveled back in time. It appeared to be his mother's town, but there were no homes. Then a group of men on horses rode up. He noticed a patch on each of their uniforms that was a symbol for the Texas Rangers. Then he observed that the main person looked like Ross Perot. Feeling anxious, he listened as the man said, "You fellers ain't from around here are you?" After that he woke up.

In examining the dream, the first symbol revealed was his mother, whom he said typified kindness. Meditation stood for relaxing into a state of self- reflection, the vortex was a centralized energy location, horses were an outdated form of transportation, Texas Rangers were authority figures and Ross Perot represented a political public authority figure, once considered viable, that became something to poke fun at because of his "loony" ways.

Helping the dreamer to understand the dream, his symbols are used in a way that will allow him to see the dream message. The message begins with feelings of inspiration and kindness. The dreamer finds a sacred place, represented by the medicine wheel, and begins to do some inner thinking with concentrated energy. Sensing a bright light, which could stand for knowledge, inspiration or transformation, the dreamer goes back in time, perhaps with his thoughts, which creates a change in his awareness. He becomes conscious of actions and ideas in his life that are connected to authority, the Texas Rangers, which no longer seem up to date. Ross Perot represents a symbol of authority that was once respected, but is no longer considered a viable action or idea.

Depending on what the dreamer was going through at the time of the dream, it may be that the he was receiving a message about change that needed to happen, or was happening, within his feelings and emotions. This awareness could only come to him at a time when he felt kindness toward himself, which was represented by the mother symbol, during a moment of mediation, a relaxing emotional state of self-reflection.

Women's Dream Symbols

A Woman's Father, Brother, Husband, Son, Imaginary Lover: The *father* in a woman's dream may symbolize her unconscious actions closely related to the things that provide for her, including actions and ideas of authority that regulate her life. In situations where there is both a stepfather and father, the father may represent closely related actions associated with kindness, love and enjoyment, while the stepfather may symbolize ideas and actions of intolerance and sternness or vice versa.

The dreamer's *brother* would represent those closely related actions and ideas that are similar to her family, actions and ideas of her heredity; whereas, the *husband* would likely represent the body of ideas and actions which she has embraced or accepted. After a woman marries she soon begins to feel the impact of her husband's many personality traits and differences in temperament due to his masculinity. The woman may have a realization that the man with whom she is living is not the person she thought him to be in her early visions of love. These visions were generally made up of her illusions about him and have been growing in her imagination through her childhood and adolescence.

It is easy for the woman to love the part of her husband that best fits her image, but she may find it much more difficult to love those aspects she did not envision. The aspects she does not understand can seem frightening and threatening. Eventually, every marriage must reach a stage of realization that while a man and woman can make one life, they still remain two individuals and each of them must deal with their own inner conflicts in their own way.

A *son* may represent hope of the future, actions and ideas not yet lived or accomplishments ready to be expressed.

The *imaginary lover* is a type of dream man who may represent the body of actions and ideas that the woman would have liked to accept, had she been able to make different choices in her life. He may also symbolize actions or ideas that she is entertaining, making love to; ideas that are difficult to consider in the conscious realm. These actions and ideas that the imaginary lover represents are usually very dear to the woman and her dream is reminding her that she wants them in her life.

Sometimes when women dream of imaginary lovers, they have a tendency to put undo demands on their husbands. A way to eliminate that challenge would be to find ways in life to experience the actions and ideas the imaginary lover represents. For example, if the imaginary lover signifies excitement, the woman may choose to find things that are creatively stimulating such as sky diving or hiking. The romantic image ceases to appear when the dreamer learns how to live her romanticized exciting actions and ideas instead of dream about them.

Dream Examples

A Husband in a Woman's Dream: I had a dream that involved two prominent men in my life, my first husband and my current husband. Each one of these men represents specific actions and ideas I have embraced. The dream began with me, three of my daughters and my first husband moving into a very large apartment. We were amazed at the size of the building and enjoyed discovering several hidden rooms. The new home represented my current structure of beliefs. Partway through the dream I realized that the action I was embracing was empty, which was represented by the awareness that we had no furniture, decorations or comforts within the home and there was nothing familiar there. In my heart I ached for my current husband, who was feeling sadness because I had chosen to move into the new structure with my first husband.

During the dream we discovered that there was a large stage or platform located in our home. I was very excited about this because we all love to perform and I knew that my family would enjoy practicing their talents on this stage. I thought it was strange that there was a man, a psychologist, speaking to a group of people on the stage in my new home. As I stood watching, pondering why he was there, I began to listen and heard him say, "It is difficult to join with two spirits, or two lives. It is difficult to embrace the two." I began to realize that I had chosen an action and idea that represented things of a materialistic nature, but my heart ached for things of a spiritual quality, which my current husband represented. I often call him my golden giant. He symbolizes sensitivity and spirituality within the current belief system I have embraced.

When I woke up from this dream, I recognized that all of my desired actions and ideas were connected unequally to things spiritual and intellectual. There are actions and ideas that have a temporal quality. They are tangible or of a material nature and there are actions and ideas which are of the spirit and intangible. The intellectual or temporal was represented by my first husband located within the unfamiliar empty home. The spiritual was represented by my current husband whom my heart ached for. Because of this dream, an awareness came to me about my goals. I had focused my goals (actions and ideas symbolized by the two men) to those of a materialistic nature, but my heart was aching for a more spiritual path. I have since altered my focus to one more sacred and balanced which has brought a greater internal sense of satisfaction and peace.

A Woman's Imaginary Lover Dream: A dream that my mother had with an imaginary companion happened in 1987 when the T.V. show "Hart to Hart" was airing. She said in her journal, "I dreamed my husband was Mr. Hart from the "Hart to Hart" show. He was wonderful, very loving and loyal. I just watched the episode where his wife Jennifer conked her head and saw an imaginary man who no one else could see. It seemed that Jonathan Hart didn't believe her, but he really did, which was proven to her in the end. I believe the dream is telling me to believe in my feelings (Jennifer Hart symbolized my mother's feelings and emotions. Jonathan Hart represented the action of loyalty). It's wonderful when our feelings, thoughts, and actions agree. This is productive and creative." The dream message was clear to her, be loyal to yourself and trust in your feelings.

A Woman's Mother, Grandmother, Sister, Daughter, Granddaughter: A woman's *mother* may represent patterns or closely related feelings and emotions she has identified within her life which express her present feelings and emotions. A woman's *sister* is closely identified with characteristics and possibilities, which the dreamer is intimately associated, someone similar to herself. Sometimes these sister symbols represent aspects of the dreamer which are usually very competitive and may resemble her own image of her unconscious problem not quite accepted in life.

When a woman gives birth to children in dreams, the birth of a son usually represents the creation of new actions and ideas. The birth of a *daughter* may symbolize the beginning of new feelings and emotions, closely related feelings and emotions that she chooses to protect and nurture. This type of dream could also be a signal concerning sentiments that represent a specific characteristic that particular daughter corresponds to.

Grandmother often represents wisdom and security. She is the ancient woman image who portrays the family patterns of feeling. Since there is often more than one grandmother, frequently of different types, ask the dreamer what this grandmother figure represents or symbolizes to them. For example, in thinking of my two grandmothers, my mom's mother creates images in my mind of industry, strength and wisdom. My father's mother represents tenderness, forgiveness and innocence.

The *grandchildren* represent a projection into the future to see traits in their purest form. When dreaming of grandchildren, the dreamer is able to see more clearly and objectively the traits they represent. Grandchildren can symbolize hidden values in relationship to our own actions and ideas, feelings and emotions. The granddaughter may even represent the woman's innate parts of her own natural tendencies.

Dream Examples

A Woman's Daughter Dream: One woman dreamed that she was telling her daughter off for complaining that her siblings didn't pay her for babysitting. The mother, being annoyed at the daughter, said, "Oh for heaven's sake! Get over it! They shouldn't have to pay you, we are a family! And getting reimbursed for gas, well that is just nonsense!" At that statement the mother looked up from what she was doing and noticed the daughter had left and the daughter's husband stood in her place. Seeing her son-in-law standing there, the woman finished speaking stating that she wanted to go home and began to pack her things, while trying to figure out just how she was going to get home. The woman's daughter represented feelings and emotions of selfishness, whining and complaining. The son-in-law symbolized actions and ideas of protection, strength, fear and darkness. Going home meant finding security.

At the time of the dream this woman had been whining about her "lot in life" and was sick and tired of her own complaining. The dream brought her to a realization that the action to change seemed dark and fearful. She just wanted to go home to where she felt secure and safe, but she needed to change her attitude about her life in order to feel the security her home represented. To change her attitude she realized the power of her words had a major affect upon her outlook and belief system. Instead of whining and complaining she created a gratitude journal and every day wrote ten things she was grateful for. By doing this her whining decreased and her heart was filled with love and appreciation.

Step Relationships

A Stepfather, stepmother, stepbrother, stepsister, step child: Dreaming of a step relationship may represent the action or idea, feeling or emotion that has stepped into the dreamer's life experience. If the term 'step' has specific meaning to the dreamer, remember to take that into consideration with the dream interpretation. The person and what they symbolize to the dreamer would be the most important thing to consider.

Even though men and women have many dream symbols that can be interpreted with the same meaning, be aware that they do have some differences of viewpoint which cause certain symbols to take on definite meanings according to whether they appear in a man or woman's dream. Remember that in life, men are primarily identified with actions and ideas and women generally are more associated with feelings and emotions.

"Lord of the world's undying youth,
What joys are in thy might!
What beauties of the inner truth,
And of the outer sight!
And when the heart is dim and sad,
Too weak for wisdom's beam,
Thou sometimes makest it right glad
With but a childish dream."
—George MacDonald

Chapter 9

Prophetic Possibilities

*"The soul, by its interior vision, may see not
only what is passing at a great distance,
but it may also know in advance what
is to happen in the future."*
—Camille Flammarion

Through all ages there have been accounts of prophetic dreams. According to the *Catholic Encyclopedia*, Marcian, Emperor of Rome at Constantinople, dreamed that he saw the bow of his great enemy, Attila the Hun, break. That same night it is reported that Attila died. In *Plutarch's Lives*, Rome's first Emperor Augustus, while ill and through the dream of a friend, was persuaded to leave his tent, which a few hours after was captured by the enemy and his bed was pierced with the enemies' swords. Tartini, a distinguished violinist, composed his *"Devil's Sonata"* under the inspiration of a dream, or semi-trance state, and Mozart, the famous Classical composer, said that composing was like being in a vivid dream.

There are dreams that could be called aspirations of foretelling that predict coming events which could affect large groups of people, perhaps even dreams whose effects could be felt worldwide. Other prophetic dreams may be personal with a type of forewarning message of crisis intended only for the dreamer. These dreams are evidence of the dreamer's ability to perceive subtle life movements which have been building in emotional tensions suggesting a possible crisis. Dreams of this manner should be interpreted based on the intimate feelings of the dreamer and objectively based on facts, to receive the valuable insights that may help the dreamer avoid or prepare for the perceived oncoming crisis.

Dreams often tell of emotional or personal dangers and may contain messages or warnings about the dreamer's actions. There are some dreams that come to caution slow change and by heeding these dream warnings the dreamer may avoid much pain and discomfort. Because prophetic dreams often leave impressions of dread or concern, they should be suspected as dreams with an intended caution. Dreams that end in a hopeless disaster frequently contain predictions for the dreamer that their life, or life values, may be lost if they continue on their present pathway. These dreams come as an admonition alerting dangers concerning greater values in life. The famine of Egypt was revealed by a vision of fat and lean cattle. The parents of Christ, being warned of the savage edict of Herod, fled with the Divine Child into Egypt. The fifth prefect of the Roman province of Judea, Pontius Pilate, was advised by his wife, who through the influence of a dream, told him to have nothing to do with the conviction of Christ.

When I was a young married mother with three children, my husband decided that he wanted to go back to live what he called his "old lifestyle". I remember experiencing feelings of anxiety about how this would affect the stability of our marriage. His idea of "old lifestyle" involved an abandon of our agreed upon religious activities. I couldn't fathom how I could possibly enjoy a marriage with this unwanted change in our relationship. It was during this time of emotional crisis that I had a vivid and profound warning dream.

The dream began with me standing at the opening of a deep, dark cavern. Feeling very concerned about my location, I noticed that a few yards away stood the devil who was dragging my husband down into the cavern. In anger and desperation I began to run after them. With rage building heavily in my soul, I was determined to rescue my husband and bring him back to safety! Then instantly I found myself standing face to face with the devil, a very handsome and charismatic being. He had thick, black curly hair, piercing deep brown-black eyes, and a strong muscular physique. Looking me squarely in the face he said, "Your husband is coming of his own free will and choice. If you choose to follow after him in your anger, you will be in my control as well." With that warning I quickly ran out of the dark cavern, outside to a place of brightness and protection. It was then that I felt the only thing capable of conquering that type of powerful evil was love.

The dream felt intensely real, like a vision, and seemed like I had literally looked into the face of evil and lived to tell about it. In analyzing this dream I could see that a warning message was being revealed. The cavern represented a dark and scary unknown world that I was facing at the time. The devil symbolized all that was corrupt and sinister as well as actions that were very appealing and enticing. I have come to realize that intense feelings of anger have certain energies or addicting powers and at times can be very alluring and energizing.

This evil had come into my life with the purpose of taking away the actions and ideas of marriage I had so dearly loved and embraced, which was represented by my husband in the dream. Coming face to face with the devil helped me realize that in my justified and emotion filled rage, I too could succumb to the darkness that he represented and be lost forever. After hearing the prophetic words of warning I understood that only love could conquer this type of experience. Actions of love were needed to save the values I held dear, values that I had embraced through marriage.

Shortly after this dream, while I was a few months pregnant with my fourth child, my mother bought plane tickets for me and my three girls so we could go to Santa Monica, California and stay with her for a month long visit. She knew I was struggling with feelings of despair and confusion, so as a type of "vacation therapy" as she called it, Mom felt it would be good for us to have some fun. She planned for us to visit some popular tourists sights and swimming at the beach.

I started this trip struggling with strong negative emotions; however, I kept remembering the impression of my dream, the feeling that love was the answer to my challenging situation. Try as I might, I wasn't able to feel love in my heart. To make matters worse I faced several incidents which tested my patience and sanity. On the first day of our visit my youngest daughter found rat poison hidden under the buffet and ate it. After calling Poison Control, I was relieved to learn that having her drink a cup of milk would keep her from experiencing much harm. I am certain that the straight pin I found her nibbling on later that evening might not have been as harmless! Then there was the event at the grocery store where I was shoved and knocked over by a man running from a police officer yelling and waving a gun. The evening excitement, when the Mercedes dealership down the street burned to the ground, with all the black smoke, sirens and crowds, will always be remembered!

The only place for me and my girls to sleep was in the attic and the heat and noise at night was almost crippling, which interfered with my much needed rest. My pregnant body missed the comfort of my own bed. Thoughts and feelings of love were far from my heart and I found myself counting the days until my girls and I could return to the pleasures of our own home.

The last week at Mom's finally arrived. We decided to take a short drive to Farmer's Market where we were determined to get a flat of strawberries. The strawberries at this particular market were deep red, plump, sweetly intoxicating and delightfully juicy. With two children in tow and one hanging onto my skirt, as well as a flat of strawberries gently resting on my little, round, pregnant belly, we slowly proceeded to the parking area. Mom had gone ahead to pull the car closer so we had less ground to cover. It was a busy underground parking lot, but she found a little spot to scoot into which allowed the traffic to go around her. We stood off to the side waiting for all the vehicles to pass before crossing the parking area to where Mom waited.

As we were getting ready to scurry over to her car, a lady in a small white vehicle pulled directly behind my mom and started honking her horn. We motioned for her to move around, but she wouldn't budge. Her incessant honking echoed wildly in that underground arena and it didn't take long for me to feel that all familiar rage rising within my soul! She finally went around Mom's car and drove off. In that instant I had a wickedly delicious thought. I glanced down at the strawberries, looked up at her car as it drove past, looked back at the flat of strawberries, then picked the fattest, juiciest strawberry I could find, and with much pleasure, threw it at her car.

Shortly after throwing the plump juicy strawberry the small white car came to a screeching halt and an angry woman, with splattered strawberry dripping down her cheek, charged toward me! I stood in the parking lot with my little children clinging to my side while this shocked and angry woman proceeded to scream at me then slap me in the face. I began to whistle and yell for the cops, which prompted her to run back to her car and drive away.

It was in that instant that I went from intense rage, to love, gratitude, humility and appreciation. How? I don't know, but I do know that I deserved the slap! This was one of the most valuable turning points of my life. It felt as though I had received a much needed spanking from God!

I was in California to find love with a strong awareness of the importance of feeling love. Thank goodness the message finally got through to my heart. I was able to go home while embracing the values of love, humility and understanding, which allowed me to be patient with my husband who needed to go through his own learning experiences.

Sometimes it is difficult to realize and incorporate the messages in emotion filled, prophetic dreams. It certainly was a challenge for me with my dream. These types of dreams may leave us with strong feelings of fear or dread and possibly emotions of confusion and frustration. Writing the dream down, paying attention to your current life situations and asking for guidance to understand the dream meaning, while being patient, can be a helpful way to see more clearly.

Another example of a prophetic dream came to my mother. Mom called one day telling me she was told in a dream that she was going to die. Analyzing the dream from every possible angle, she just became more confused. Feeling healthy and happy, she had created some exciting personal goals for herself and had recently moved to a small town that she loved and enjoyed. Mom called to ask for my help in the interpretation of the dream, because it felt peculiar to her.

I distinctly remember my feelings after she told me her dream and knew that it was a prophetic dream, feeling certain that she was going to die soon. I felt it was best to keep my thoughts private during our discussions. We never came to a clear interpretation of her dream, nor did we talk about it again, but every time the phone rang

I thought it would be a message that my mother had died. A year after her dying dream mom passed away. Sometimes I think that my mother didn't understand her dream, because the dream was a message for me so that I would be prepared for her transition from this life to the next. Perhaps she did know and understand the dream meaning, but just couldn't bring herself to acknowledge and accept the message.

My mother's dream did not feel prophetic to her, just strange and confusing. By taking an objective view of the dream, I could see that because she had recently moved to a new area and had a change in her life style, with the loss of familiar friends and associates, her dream could represent a type of death or an end to life as she knew it. That could have been the dream's warning and nothing more. Nevertheless, when she told me the dream she talked about it as if it were prophetic by certain words that she used. She repeatedly said, "I don't think I am going to die! I feel better than I ever have!" She never once talked to me about it being a message other than a warning of death. Her feelings of good health and the fear of dying were possible causes for her confusion. This is a classic example of a dream that should be interpreted objectively as well as prophetically in order to receive the valuable insights that may help the dreamer to avoid or prepare for the perceived oncoming crisis.

Dreaming of disasters and frightening events, which fortunately don't always come true, are experienced by many people. So how does one know if the dream is prophetic or not? In dreams, impressions or intuitions from spirit, God or Divine source, who is the highest personal communicator of intelligence, can be received. By studying these impressions that come through the soul language into dreams, and by living lives in harmony with the universal mind, it is possible to shape the future in accordance to spiritual law and receive the necessary guidance to understand the dream message.

Chapter 10

Gifts of the Spirit

"And it shall come to pass afterward, that I will
pour out my spirit upon all flesh; and your sons and
your daughters shall prophecy, your
old men shall dream dreams,
your young men shall see visions:"
—Joel 2:28

A wise man once said that visions are gifts of the spirit. Through visions, knowledge is revealed from source. In the Old Testament there are several recorded visions of the prophet Isaiah foretelling the ministry and sufferings of Jesus of Nazareth. The Book of Revelations, comprised of a wonderful symbolic language containing scores of symbols and images, reveals John's visions of the risen Lord, the throne of God, fire, desolation, plagues and winged beasts full of eyes! From the Bible, Ezekiel shares his visions of the divine warrior in his battle chariot, God enthroned in the temple surrounded by heavenly beings and the valley of dry bones.

Joan of Arc, heroine of France and a Roman Catholic Saint, claimed to have seen and talked with angels. Goethe, writer and politician, witnessed his own self coming toward him on horseback on the same road as he was traveling, in attire that he had never worn. He claimed that his manifestation was not experienced from the body, but from the mind. Several years after the experience he found himself on that very road dressed in the attire of his vision.

In the narrations of "The Dream of a Painter," Sir Joshua Reynolds, English painter from the 1700s, narrates an experience he had with an angelic visitor. Several early masters of the arts were shown to him in vision including Leonardo da Vinci, skilled Italian artist, and Raphael, Italian painter and architect. In the early 1800s, after reading the Epistle of James, first chapter and fifth verse, "If any of you lack wisdom, let him ask of God, that giveth to all men liberally, and upbraideth not; and it shall be given him," a young boy named Joseph, who desired to receive wisdom from his Divine source, knelt in private prayer and offered up the feelings of his heart. It was during that prayer through a glorious vision that he received his answer.

Christopher Columbus, famous Italian explorer whose voyages led to the first permanent European contact with the Americas, had a dream during one of his most difficult ocean trips. While restless in sleep a merciful voice was heard chastising him to have trust and not fear. The message was a comfort for him during a time of great difficulty.

Much like dreams, visions as gifts of the spirit are messages sent to guide and direct the soul on its journey. Manifestations may present themselves as a stream of light bringing knowledge while touching the mind with an increased mental awareness. There may be instances when a voice is heard, an impression is felt or a vivid image is witnessed. How or when a vision will manifest is often unknown; however, most visionary experiences usually come during times of quiet prayer and meditation. In Psalms, chapter forty six verse ten, it is written, "Be still and know that I am God." Remember those words when asking for guidance.

Dream Visions

When he was 18 years old, my husband had a dream in which he was sitting on a soft, dirty couch, holding a large three ring binder sideways like a flip-chart and teaching a teenage boy about how we were all spirits before we were born. The room was lit primarily by a large fish tank with lights on the top shining down into the water. The fish tank was making a loud bubbly noise and there was a musty smell. At the time of the dream, he was living in Flagstaff, Arizona. Approximately six months later, he was in Binghamton, New York and found himself sitting on that soft, dirty couch, holding the flip-chart, talking and hearing the bubbles from the fish tank. "Everything was the same, down to the tiniest detail". The young man he was teaching was named Jim.

My husband had never experienced anything like that before and has not had a similar experience since. About a year after that, he attended Jim's grandfather's funeral. A story was told at the funeral, which all of the children and grandchildren were aware of because it had been told to them as part of their parents and grandparents lives. When Jim's grandpa was 12 years old, he was attending a dance and felt the need to leave the small building and go outside for a breath of fresh air. He exited the building and sat down on some stairs, while sitting there fully awake, he experienced a vision of a woman giving birth to a baby girl. This was in the early 1900s and he "had never seen anything like that". He saw the birth in detail from the doctor's perspective with all of the blood and "gory details" and could see that the baby was a girl. The vision was a shocking traumatic experience for him and he went home that night and wrote about it in detail in his journal. Sixteen years later, Jim's grandpa met a cute 16 year old girl and they began seeing each other. As they shared details of their lives, they found that she was being born when he was having the vision. That story was passed down as part of the story of "how grandpa and grandma met". My husband believes that Jim inherited a spiritual gift from his grandfather and that he was somehow able to share in that gift through the dream he had in Flagstaff.

An intuitive friend of mine had a dream vision one night where she found herself in a house that was unfamiliar yet it was suppose to be her house. "I was in my bed and a young man, I think his name was Ryan, came into my room. He was worried and was pacing at the foot of my bed. I wasn't sure who he was, although it felt like I knew him in some way, and I wasn't afraid of him. He told me that his family wasn't being realistic and that his time was near. He wanted me to give him Reiki and comfort him to help him on his path. He also wanted me to promise that I would help his parents deal with losing him. I asked if he wanted to lie on the bed next to me, which he did. I was under the covers and he was resting on top of them. I put my hand on his chest and as he closed his eyes he took a deep breath and sighed. He told me it felt so warm and good and comforting. He was quiet for a short time and I just kept my one hand, right hand, on the middle of his chest. I was lying on my left side watching him. Then he smiled, but kept his eyes closed and he told me not to worry, that my grandsons love me and they will come to me in Divine time."

The dreamer specifically stated that this felt like a vision more than a dream. When she woke up she still felt Ryan's presence. It was early when she woke up, around the same time that her spirit guide often woke her giving her a message to remember for that day. When we discussed the dream and its possible symbols, one symbol in particular jumped out at her. The name Ryan means "Little King" which has a strong symbolic meaning to the dreamer. She felt good about the dream as a vision and any message she needed to hear was privately understood and received.

A Guiding Force

A man in his mid-thirty's was investigating different religions trying to decide which one to join. He investigated one particular religion for over two years and liked many things about it, but was not comfortable with actually joining. One day he was sitting in his easy chair and a vision opened up "like the iris of a camera". He saw a bearded, barefoot man in white robes, who looked him in the eyes, then slowly turned away from him and stepped up on a rock. The vision closed in the same manner as it opened. The man believed that the person he saw was Jesus Christ. He interpreted the vision as a message that he should join the religion he had been studying. The man, his two daughters and wife have experienced many years of happiness fully embracing the teachings and social structure of that church.

While reviewing current events in my life, my children with their growth and independence, my husband and his personal influence and my path as a woman in her mid-fifties experiencing life's physical and emotional changes, I was taught through a vision. The message came when I was resting during the in between moments of sleep and awareness. I heard myself saying, "I am lost and not sure which way I should go." In that instant I saw an imposingly handsome Native American brave sitting on a majestic black stallion. The brave had three feathers in his headband, long, straight, dark brown hair, and appeared to be about forty years of age. Sitting tall on his stallion he just looked at me. He was alone positioned on a rocky plateau that was surrounded by massive red rock formations in a large open space. The vision ended as quickly as it arrived and I sat feeling stunned at what I had seen. I began searching the internet to learn the symbolism of a Native American brave. Upon noticing my search, my husband said, "He symbolizes what he means to you." I thought, "Of course that is true," then I heard the words "freedom and strength." Through the message of the vision I realized that at this time in my life I have the freedom to do whatever I desire and I have the strength to succeed in all my undertakings.

A famous psychic once made a comment about spirit having its own agenda. This agenda is not always the same as the dreamer's. Hopefully in time all people will come to learn and understand that agenda. Two personal visions taught me the importance of listening to and following spirit's agenda.

Several years ago when my husband at the time was hired for a new job, we were staying at his parent's home until we found a house of our own. While I was deep in thought looking through a newspaper for a place to live, I experienced a vision presented as an image of a scroll unwinding. A scene appeared in the middle of the scroll showing a small manufactured home park. This specific place was forty miles away from where my husband's new job was located. Spirit revealed that this was the place we were to live. I knew it, but I certainly didn't like the message and dismissed it without further thought.

After weeks of unsuccessful in-town house searching, we conceded to the message in the vision, drove the forty miles to the manufactured home park, and had immediate success in purchasing a home. Our children felt that living that far in the middle of "no-where" was like living in a prison and I have to admit that the first few days of living there were traumatic, even for me! The closest store was forty miles away and it was a small grocery market. To do any major grocery shopping we had to travel seventy-five miles west or one-hundred twenty miles east. Church was thirty miles west and school, well, we home-schooled. There was not much hope for a social life!

Sometimes I wondered why I had that vision and why we needed to live out in the middle of "no-where". In hindsight I can see that without the vision we never would have moved forty miles away from my husband' job. In this little place called Oasis, the air was clean, the water pure; it was a healing place. Together as a family we talked, walked, played, and ate together. We became avid star gazers, board and card game pro's and creative geniuses. It was in the middle of "no-where" that our oldest daughter met her husband whom we all love and appreciate. In this place of "no-where", designed specifically for us as part of spirit's agenda for our lives, we developed strong and loving relationships. Difficult as it was at times I am grateful for that experience. It provided us with opportunities for personal growth and development according to spirit's agenda.

My children have strong soul essence vibrations. Their energy streams are intensely apparent to me because of the mother-child relationship. One of my daughters is a guardian angel essence. She has a deep connection to the earth; however, there was a time in her life when I was concerned about her choices.

During a moment of anxiety for her welfare I took the opportunity to meditate as a way of calming my fears. While in this state of meditation I had a teaching vision where I saw a young woman, who was my daughter, lying on the ground in what looked like a well tended garden. There were tall green ferns, soft, dainty flowers and thick, dark green moss covering the garden floor. Looking at my daughter with concern I watched as Mother Earth came forth out of the ground behind her. The image of Mother Earth was shown as a stunningly beautiful woman with long, golden brown hair that fell over her body in soft waves. While lying beside my daughter, Mother Earth embraced her, then smiling at me, said, "I will take care of her." I started to interrupt thinking that it was my duty as a mother to care for my own daughter. She looked at me again with a stern expression on her face, shook her head and said, "No. I will take care of her."

The vision was a gift of the spirit with an important message. By stepping out of my daughter's life, letting her deal with her choices and by trusting in spirit, my daughter has grown into an amazing young woman. I no longer worry about her and have faith that her needs are being met with love through spirit.

The Reiki Experience

Reiki, founded by Mikao Usui, is a type of complementary therapy for different ailments. In this healing technique a facilitator channels energy into a client (the receiver), by means of touch to assist with the natural healing process of the body. Reiki helps the body achieve a deep state of relaxation so that healing is possible, often restoring the body to physical and emotional wellness. Using focused intention for well-being, and while asking for the universal life force to help with the healing process, insight and visions may sometimes manifest during a Reiki session.

While doing Reiki on a woman in her early thirties I had the vision of a parasitic serpent which was located in her solar plexus and base chakra areas. The serpent started out small then gradually got bigger, winding its way down through her abdomen. As I asked for spirit to dislodge the apparition it became angry. Barring sharp fangs, its mouth gaping wide with black eyes glaring at me, it resisted the light and energy; however, after some difficulty it withdrew. The dark energy eventually released from the woman's spine, but was still present in her body causing occasional illness and discomfort. Something else needed to be done to dispel the negative energy within her.

As we discussed the vision the woman told me that for three months she had been suffering from constant illness and she was tired of it! Because of the vision, she received an inspirational message which suggested that something in her home was making her sick. She felt prompted to clean and purify her house. After physically cleaning her home, she energetically cleaned by imagining a large ball of white light resting in her palms. The light began to expand radiating through the entire space of her home, expelling any darkness that might be living there. After doing the cleansing she began to mend and regain her health. Spirit inspired her through the vision letting her know that she needed to take specific action in order for her body to heal.

A fellow Reiki practitioner and I often exchange Reiki sessions. During one of these sessions while receiving Reiki, I had a vision. With my eyes shut and relaxing energy flowing through me, I saw a large granite boulder come into my awareness with the number 24 etched deeply into the center of the stone. The vision only lasted a split second, but it astounded me!

During the weeks that led to my receiving this Reiki, I had been questioning my path and felt unsure that the direction I was focusing on was the right one for me. During the Reiki session my thoughts were once again turned toward my path. After relating the vision to my friend and fellow Reiki practitioner, I asked her what the number 24 might possibly mean, for it meant nothing symbolically to me. She felt prompted to search her angel book of numbers, and to our surprise and gratitude we learned from the book that the angel number 24 held a symbolic message encouraging me to continue on my present path with passion and enthusiasm. This was another vision with an inspiring message in answer to an inner prayer.

Being Still

One beautiful spring day my husband and I enjoyed a pleasant time at the creek. While sitting on a smooth, slightly mossy boulder, we watched the creek as it wound its way down the canyon. My husband asked me to notice how still the water was where we were sitting, yet further downstream there were jagged boulders and rough waters. He tossed a small pebble into the still waters. We watched as the ripples began to spread in all directions like energy expanding outward. Then he threw a pebble into the rough waters. We witnessed no evidence that a pebble had been tossed there. He asked, "What do these pebbles in the creek remind you of Laina? What life experiences can you relate to what you have just seen here?" He continued, "So many times we pray and search for answers to life's challenges and problems only to hear nothing. Our life's current is too swift, our emotions sensitive and sharp and our feelings are rough blocking the ability to hear. If we would just take time to 'still' ourselves like the still waters of the creek, we would be able to receive the answers."

During some of my quiet moments I have received impressions or "flashes" of knowledge, as my doctor calls them. These impressions can also be referred to as "aha moments" that are sent as light and knowledge meant to guide and teach. During one moment of stillness and contemplation I asked a few personal questions and, to my delight, I received answers.

Q: What is guilt?

A: Guilt is a reason for non change. The guilt justifies our actions allowing them to continue

Q: What is charity? I have read that charity never fails so what is it that never fails?

A: If you have done all that you can do to fix a problem or challenge you are facing, then feel love, be love, send love, see love, talk love. Charity is love. Love never fails.

Q: What is the purpose of frustration?

A: Frustration is like birth pains. You struggle to change yet you know it is necessary. You feel the push to make things happen with the work involved and the pressure of the moment. You feel pain, you cry and for a while you are angry and afraid. All of these feelings and emotions are sometimes necessary to push through to a new birth. You know you need to grow and learn. Remember that it is important to throw out the old, clean up and make ready for the new life. The birth of a new idea, feeling and emotion, action and idea, is very similar to a woman getting ready for the birth of a child. Near the time of birth she will often begin to throw out old unused items and clean the home as she gets ready for the birth. Then the real work begins as she feels the contractions, the pain, the pushing and finally the release! Like a mother feels love toward her child, treat your new birth in the same way, with love. Nurture it, embrace it, seek to understand and celebrate it!

After an embarrassing moment one day I asked,

Q: Why do we have embarrassing moments like these? What is their purpose?

A: Embarrassing moments are from the ego Laina. Humility is from Divine source.

Recording and Interpreting Visions

One of my favorite scriptures is Proverbs chapter three verses five and six, "Trust in the Lord with all thine heart; and lean not unto thine own understanding. In all thy ways acknowledge him, and he shall direct thy path." Trust in Divine source. Because gifts of the spirit are often forgotten, write down impressions and answers received. Put them in a visions journal and review them regularly.

It is important to write down visions along, with any events that may have prompted them to occur, because these events are often significant and relevant. Much like a dream, the vision may be given in an effort to solve or represent a problem, as a warning voice or in answer to a heartfelt question. Use a separate journal for dreams, a different journal for visions, one for personal history, a journal for gratitude and one for goals, etc… By using separate books, the information recorded will be much easier to access later when needed.

Chapter 11

Once Upon a Time

"All that we see or seem is but a dream within a dream."
- Edgar Allan Poe

Stories in Dreams

*E*ach dream presents insight. Some dreams may come just to clarify former interpretations of other dreams. Often there are repeat dream settings because that specific place may have held special meaning. Sometimes a single dream will present and solve a problem without any further dreams. If the dream is in a series as part of an ongoing story, the dream takes on additional significance and carries much greater meaning than a single unrelated dream.

Think of a single unrelated dream with a simple message as a short story presenting one problem. Dreams that are given as a "sequence of dreams" over several days, weeks or months, could be considered chapters in a book that reveal prevailing problems caused by inner conflicts constructed from recurrent dilemmas of a lifetime. This "sequence of dreams" is like any other ongoing story which has an introduction, body and conclusion. The introduction reveals the time, setting and the characters. The body contains the movement toward the crisis and its climax. The conclusion shows the reconstruction of life values and the embracing of more mature values.

The following is an example of a specific dream sequence shared to me by a young woman in her early thirties. I have outlined her dreams in book format to assist with seeing an introduction, body and conclusion. When recording dreams of this nature, only share them with someone who is trustworthy. These types of dreams are most often extremely sacred.

The Introduction

Introduction dreams say, "This story is worth reading." These dreams are often happy and enjoyable to the dreamer because there are glimmers of the possibility of help and feelings that there is some hope of a solution to the problem. They are dreams that indicate a wish to continue habitual thinking and feeling.

This introduction dream happened to a woman whom we will call Alice. She was struggling with a new life situation. "My family and some close friends were going to stay at a plush resort for a fun and exciting vacation. I was there along with my step-dad, my best friend with her husband and kids, my sister and her boys, and my husband and our children. While walking through the resort going up to our various suites, laughing, joking around and talking about how much fun we were going to have, we noticed the swimming pool was empty of water. Then all at once everyone in our group noticed two zombies in the pool! The zombies smelled of death with decomposed flesh rotting from their limbs. As soon as I looked at the pool and saw the zombies I knew we needed to hurry to our rooms to be safe. When I looked at the pool again it was filled to the top with rotting zombies, then all of a sudden we were safely in our rooms. Everyone realized that the entire resort was inundated with crazed zombies! We knew that in order to get out of the resort safely it would be necessary to stay close together. As we were going out to dinner, walking on a higher level looking down to the reception area, again we saw that the resort was overflowing with zombies! Even some of the rooms were full of zombies. We stuck together and we were safe."

After discussing the symbols and their meanings with the dreamer, she realized that in order to survive her perceived current life dangers, some of which she said, "Seemed almost empty and void of life, symbolized by the creatures (life actions) that could eat me alive," it would be necessary for her to remain secure. She could feel this security by staying close to the things she valued most, her closely related actions and ideas, feelings and emotions, represented in the dream by close family and friends.

The Body

Once the initial resistance in any problem is overcome, the dreamer then plunges into the action of the story. This is the frightening and exciting part, but also the place of dread, fear and suspense. In many instances these dreams manifest themselves as nightmares to the dreamer. The residue of such dreams is often to awaken trembling, trying to cry out or in tears, for the dreamer is dealing with deeply emotional material.

Among the first dreams in the body of the emotional story are those that show the dreamer's fear of facing hidden conflicts. These dreams help in choosing whether to continue or to pause and rest a while. They show the degree of resistance that must be overcome before daring to enter the realm of shadows which can be filled with suppressed or dreaded emotions and memories.

Dreams which picture the entrance into the feared experience of a crisis use many images to depict their message. These images could be scenes of going through cemeteries, vaults or tombs. Some people dream of coffins where the corpse moves or shows signs of life. No matter how deeply people think they have buried their emotions, they are not dead and can and will be resurrected. In Karol Truman's book *Feelings Buried Alive Never Die,* she teaches that if feelings are left unresolved, the energy of these emotions remain inside growing and expanding, gathering more energy the longer they are ignored. Eventually these expanding energies create a block which can negatively affect the body. By becoming aware of these affects, positive changes will begin to appear.

During revealing dreams, situations dealing with animal instincts may appear. Many different animal figures may manifest ranging from spiders to elephants. Other symbols that appear could be long halls with doors on each side, menacing beasts or big, angry, incarcerated men, murders, thieves and kidnappers. People wade through swamps, struggle in whirlpools or dream of half submerged dungeons and other forms of waters. When the individual is experiencing this deep dream sequence they need the close cooperation and help of someone trustworthy who can help them with the dream interpretation.

Alice, who experienced the introduction dream with the zombies, received a crisis dream as part of the body in her dream sequencing. The dream began with her trying to escape a monsoon rainstorm with such a torrential downpour that cars were falling off cliffs and people were dying all around her. As she stood by the side of her car which was at the edge of a dangerous cliff, she realized that she needed to open the passenger side door to get in safely. Alice chose to get in the driver's side instead, the side which was dangerously close to the edge of the cliff. If the car fell over the cliff she knew that she would fall into a swirling whirlpool at the bottom of the ravine and die. Knowing this, Alice still tried to put her key in the driver side door and climb in.

After a few moments of intense fear and frustration, she looked down and noticed a locket on the ground which represented all that remained of her marriage. There was something inscribed on the locket, but she couldn't read it and could not remember what the inscription was. Alice began to sob. Her friends, family and husband were lost down in the swirling whirlpool below. She felt that she was going to die and didn't know how to save herself!

When someone dreams about water, this often symbolizes the great unconscious where all ideas, emotions and actions spring. By the form the water takes in dreams and a person's relationship to it, the dreamer can determine what the unconscious is trying to reveal. In this young woman's dream, it is revealed that she was experiencing an emotional storm of such an extent that she felt confused and devastated by all she had lost. The things she valued most as her actions and ideas were symbolized by her husband and male associates. Her feelings and emotions were symbolized by her children and other important female connections. During the dream analysis she said that everyone was gone, they were all dead. They had all died in the storm and were in the whirlpool below her. She also mentioned that the locket was the link to her understanding why and how she was connected to her husband. The locket was all that was left of their marriage. She showed extreme frustration in her inability to remember what that link was.

We discussed why she chose to go to the driver's side to get in the car knowing that doing so could cause her death. While evaluating her reasons for making that choice she realized that her subconscious was telling her to let go of the driving, let go of the control and allow herself to be a passenger until she reached a place of security. I mentioned that she would probably receive a conclusion dream showing the ascent, a way to a new life and all was not lost. She still held the chain, the subconscious symbol revealed as a locket that connected her to marriage, togetherness, a joining of the elements, a link to her new life. She recognized that ultimately she would remember the message on the locket and experience pleasure and eventually regain control of her life.

The Conclusion

Conclusion dreams show that the abyss has really been experienced and the dreamer is ready to ascend into a new way of life. These dreams involve finding a lost key, moving into a new house, fixing up an old one, seeing green growing things, riding a horse, driving a car, finding buried treasure, traveling to foreign lands, the birth of a child or any type of dream where the dreamer regains the control of their emotions and life.

Not long after the crisis dream of the storm and whirlpool, Alice had another dream, her ascent dream, part of the conclusion in her dream series. She found herself experiencing what she said was a type of recurring dream in a place she had visited before. After walking around the section of an older town with little shops and cafés, hotels and antique stores, the young woman discovered a quaint and inviting shop filled with sweet, decadent chocolates, moist, mouthwatering cakes and other tempting and delicious goodies.

The interior of the shop was white, not too white though, but clean and pure. To see the goodies in the glass cases she had to look down at a slight angle. The lady behind the counter was beautiful with long, silky blond hair, a full length flowing skirt, modest jewelry and a sweet gentle smile. She was feminine and delicate, but physically powerful and had a strong intuitive sense of knowing exactly what type of goodies her customers needed. The lady handed Alice a scrumptious looking, vanilla raspberry cookie. Alice seemed to automatically know that to get the best flavor out of the cookie before eating it, she needed to hold it to her pulse first, just under her ear on her neck, which she did, and discovered that the cookie was satisfyingly delicious!

After eating her cookie, Alice noticed some coconut macaroons, one of her favorite goodies. She saw pastel purple macaroons, and pink delicate teal ones too, and said, "They were really good. It was surprisingly enjoyable to be in that place and I was excited to be there. I just knew I wanted those macaroons." She proceeded to fill a box full of goodies to take home, then had a thought that it was going to be expensive, but decided she didn't care and bought the treats anyway. "It was worth it."

Before this conclusion dream appeared, Alice had chosen to change her belief system through prayer. "I decided to change the way I prayed. I started asking for help in loving others, as well as help to live my life the way the Lord wanted me to live. One day I noticed a friend of mine whose kids were disrespectful and rude. They didn't obey her and they showed little or no gratitude toward their mother. As I thought about my friend's children I realized that my children were respectful, obedient and loving. While my young teenage step-daughter was following me around one day I had the impression to tell her of my appreciation. My first impulse was, "No way, I'm not telling her that," but the impression stayed with me. Finally, I could stand it no longer and I told her how much she meant to me, how I loved her, and how pleased I was to have her in my life. We both cried and hugged. It was a choice and treasured moment."

After discussing her dream, its symbols and their meanings, the young woman realized she had discovered the link (locket), which was manifested as gratitude. This link of gratitude brought her to a more enjoyable life. She began to feel the excitement and love that she thought had so traumatically been taken from her. No longer needing to be in control, she had chosen to let divine spirit guide her and found it to be delicious and very satisfying. Gratitude is the pulse of life. She said "It was worth the price I had to pay to get here!"

Summary

When a degree of self acceptance has taken place, the individual's mind is freed from some of its emotional blocks and confusions. New ideas can then come to consciousness. Don't be alarmed if there are occasional dreams which refer to former phases. These dreams will add insights that were possibly overlooked. The previously rejected self will now begin to pour out its wisdom and energy using many images to illustrate age old truths. These will be helpful images such as fairies, prophets, folklore stories, angels, the wise old man and perhaps a feminine, powerful woman with silky blond hair.

Educational dreams will come throughout life. When a problem needs to be solved a dream may come pointing out the reason for the problem and perhaps its solutions. Sometimes it may take many dreams before the unconscious messages are fully understood. Some will seem very plain because they are educational dreams. Other dreams may be starting a new sequence and therefore be more confusing, but experience with interpretations will help to unravel each new sequence with more understanding.

Chapter 12

The Art of Reverie

"Don't only practice your art, but force your way into it's secrets. For it and knowledge can raise men to the divine."
—Ludwig Van Beethoven

Reverie is a state of being pleasantly lost in thought, a type of day-dream or distraction of thoughts from the present moment. It is a point in time where the mind lets the imagination wander. During day-dreaming the psyche can solve problems, come up with answers to difficult questions or be a doorway to creativity. When teaching my children during home school, I noticed that when one of my daughters would get frustrated while learning a new concept, the best course of action in assisting her was to give her a mindless task to perform. She would often go to her room and clean or write poetry. Invariably, after a few minutes of doing this, she would come back to her schoolwork with greater understanding and solve the problem that she had previously struggled with. This type of mindless action, or what I call "organized day-dreaming", helped her to get the best use of her brain power.

"I think; Therefore I am," is a famous quote by the French philosopher Rene Descartes. He thought of day-dreams as a form of higher mental awareness. There are many famous day-dreamers in history, people who used this type of mental awareness to benefit humanity. When he was sixteen years of age, Albert Einstein imagined traveling with a light beam. While sleeping he felt himself travel on a ray of the sun to the edge of the universe and back. This visual imagination of motion would later result in the theory of relativity. Mozart said, "All this inventing, this producing, takes place in a lively dream." Thomas Edison use to sit in a chair with a heavy weight in one hand and day-dream. When he would drift off in sleep, the weight would fall out of his hand making a loud sound on the ground which would arouse him. Then he would write down all he had been day-dreaming about during that moment. Leonardo da Vinci, well known painter, engineer, sculptor, musician, writer, scientist and architect, would look at walls and visualize never-ending images of people and scenery.

Vitruvius, a Roman architect in the first century BC, told the story of Archimedes who uncovered fraud in the making of a golden crown. Hiero II, who had commissioned the making of the golden crown, suspected that the goldsmith may have replaced some of the gold by an equal weight of silver. Hiero asked Archimedes to determine whether the crown was pure gold. While

Archimedes entered the public bath, he noticed the more his body entered the water, the more water ran out of the tub. This observation provided a way for him to explain the case in question. Being excited at this realization, he promptly jumped out of the tub and ran home naked, shouting those famous words, "Eureka, eureka," which in Greek means "I have found it. I have found it!"

Brahms, a famous German composer and pianist, claimed that spirit is universal and is the, "Creative energy of the Cosmos." He felt that in order to grow people must learn to develop their own soul forces. Strauss, another leading German composer, felt that when inspiration came while composing, he was tapping into the source of Infinite and Eternal energy. Many other great composers like Brahms and Strauss felt that they were partners with the creator in their composing. Puccini claimed that all creative geniuses drew on the same omnipotent power. He felt that it was through this divine influence that he was able to create his greatest works. He related inspiration to a type of awakening which can manifest itself in high achievements.

By learning from these great examples throughout history, and by allowing the mind to tap into the omnipotent power and receive inspiration, a wonderful tool can be used to stimulate divinely inspired creativity. Along the lines of day-dreaming and tools which stimulate creativity, there is an art called creative visualizing. With creative visualizing a person may begin to realize their ambitions through focused mental imagery. When becoming more aware of symbolic communications in dreams, the question may arise concerning recurring life situations. There is a message in recurring situations that can be realized by paying attention to day-dreams. Ask, "What am I thinking about when I drift into a day-dream? Am I consciously aware of my thoughts? Could my thoughts be influencing my path, my recurring life situations or my dreams?" By paying attention to thoughts and day-dreams, creating a life of conscious choice may begin to come into focus.

Science has proven that through specific sustained intentions, humans are capable of influencing their environment. In the book *The Intention Experiment* by Lynn Ann McTaggert, there is information about an experiment performed by physicist William Tiller. Tiller developed a device that could measure energy produced by healers. While standing a few inches from the device, volunteers were told to focus on a specific mental intention which was then measured by the device in pulses. Even intentions that were sent by participants from a distance created a change in pulses. From this experiment Tiller discovered that when thoughts are directed, physical energy is produced. According to other studies shared in McTaggert's book, electrical and magnetic energy may manifest through focused intention producing an ordered stream of protons. Creative focus is the beginning process of ordering protons. I call this process of ordering protons "creative visualizing."

Practicing the Art of Day-dreaming as Creative Visualizing

The famous writer and politician Johann Wolfgang von Goethe once said, "Whatever you can do, or dream you can, begin it. Boldness has genius, power and magic in it."

There are several successful techniques to the creative dream process. These techniques can have a magical influence on life. The following are just a few suggestions for creative visualizing:

Suggestion one: Find a quiet place of comfort to relax and enjoy relative privacy. In our home we have a comfortable chair in our bedroom, a designated place where we can go to enjoy the creative process. Energy vibrates at the frequency of desires. By choosing a specific place to relax and imagine, this oscillating energy remains in that space over a period of time. In the book *Conscious Acts of Creation, The Emergence of a New Physics,* the authors call this a conditioning of space. My husband often meditates in a small soft rocking chair located in our living room. He occasionally falls asleep during his day-dreaming meditations. We find it amusing to watch our guests when they come to visit. Periodically someone will sit in the meditation chair. After a few minutes in this conditioned space they either enter into a state of total relaxation or fall asleep. It is a plain, old, little rocking chair, but it quickly becomes our visitor's favorite place to sit!

Suggestion two: Have a specific goal in mind. Several times in my life I have used day-dreaming with creative visualizing to manifest a new home. I begin by seeing myself walking up the front pathway, climbing the stairs to my porch and entering the front door. As I do this, I notice the flowers in my yard, birds and other pleasures of nature, the color of my home, the sounds of the area and anything that makes the day-dream feel real and in present moment. Sometimes I write in a journal about my new home experiences as if the occurrences really happened, this is writing in present time. I feel happy in the dream, smell the scents and listen to the sounds that could be in my new home. I imagine experiencing the physical sensations of actually being there and infuse the vision with as much emotion as possible. There is a Hindu proverb that states, "Man is a creature of reflection; he becomes that upon which he reflects." When I reflect, I am in my thoughts in great detail with feelings of joy and satisfaction! I become part of the vision.

Suggestion three: Let go of the outcome. Enjoy the moment, let the vision take its course and believe the action will happen. Doing this brings about enjoyment in day-dreaming while allowing the creative process to manifest when and how the universe chooses to reveal the creation. There are several wonderful books written about day-dreaming, goals and creative visualizing. Read these books and practice some of the techniques that resonate through the soul.

Be in gratitude for each moment of life while dreaming and creating. Remember the teaching in the book *Parable of the Hand and the Glove* by Allen Smithson which states that NOW is an "Amazingly delightful place and time to live."

Chapter 13
Good Night, Sleep Tight

"In a dream, in a vision of the night, when deep sleep falleth
upon men, in slumberings upon the bed; then he openeth
the ears of men and sealeth their instruction, that he may
withdraw man from his purpose, and hide pride from man."
—Job 33:15-17

Recording Your Dreams

It is important to find a process of recording dreams that will be a comfortable and standard method to use. In the beginning it is good to get the dreams on paper as accurately as possible. Some individuals speak their dreams into a recording device and write them down later. This should be done in a simple and non stressful way. I suggest having a designated book especially for dreams that can be referenced easily.

The dream is like an autobiography of the dreamer revealing how they feel, disclosing a type of uncensored, emotional truth. These truths are made known through symbols. If the symbols are not understood the first time, the mind will create a new set of dreams with different symbols to assist with achieving a better understanding of the message that needs to be revealed.

In order to better comprehend what certain symbols personally mean, begin establishing a dream dictionary. Start the dream dictionary alphabetically and fill the sections with symbols that appear in dreams. Write down feelings about each particular symbol at that time. Some dreamers use a 3x5 alphabetized card file, others use an address book and some create a computerized file system. This should be something that is easy to reference while proceeding with dream interpreting.

Once it has been established what personal symbols represent, begin inserting them into the written dream. Place the symbols in a way that is easiest to read and understand. For example, I had the following dream and as I wrote it down I added the symbol's meanings: "I was in my kitchen, (a place of joy and comfort) when I noticed that hundreds (many) of sugar ants (irritations, things that annoy) were all around me!" This bothered me immensely because I just wanted to cook and enjoy myself! In my personalized dream dictionary sugar ants symbolize pesky things that irritate and annoy, my kitchen is a place to create while experience joy. Upon awakening I realized that I was letting the little pesky and irritating things in my life bother me which influenced my joy.

The dream brought me to an awareness of what I was unconsciously doing. Because of the dream message I chose to change my reactions toward the pesky things around me to thoughts and feelings of understanding, patience, acceptance and tolerance. Doing this brought back my joy!

The Final Sentences

While recording dreams, pay attention to the final sentences. These usually awaken the dreamer because they are so vital that the conscious imagination grabs on to their message thus grabbing the dreamer's attention. The main message of the dream may also be revealed in the last sentence of the dream. Once awake, notice the type of emotion the dream created. These emotions may be as important as any symbols in the dream. They may help to verify emotions felt in the dream; however, sometimes they may consciously contradict those very feelings. Also, take note of the time frame of the dream. Dreaming of things from childhood could be a message that the challenges currently being faced in life began back in childhood.

One of my clients related a dream to me that had an ending where the final sentence reminded her of a traumatic time in her life. The dream began with her and her husband at the movie theater. When she sat down to enjoy the movie, amniotic water gushed out of her! Jumping up she exclaimed, "Honey, my water just broke! We need to go to the hospital." When they arrived at the hospital emergency room, she began sharing her surprise with the paramedics about being pregnant. She related to the attendants that she was fifty-nine, had no uterus and their daughter was seventeen.

In analyzing this dream we began with what the

dream symbols meant to her. The symbols' meanings are in parenthesis in her dream analysis. The dreamer and her husband (actions and ideas that she has embraced and loves) are at the movie theater (a place of entertainment where you enjoy a story that is watched, not read). When she sat down in her seat, amniotic water (serenity) gushed out of her! She jumped up and said "Honey, my water just broke! We need to go to the hospital!" (a place to be taken care of in hopes of getting better). When they arrived at the hospital emergency room (a place to get help and hopefully get better) she began sharing her surprise at being pregnant (new life). She related to the attendants that she was fifty-nine and had no uterus (no more productivity) and their daughter was seventeen.

In talking with the dreamer I learned that at the age of seventeen her daughter went through a traumatic event that drastically changed her life, as well as that of the dreamer. The final sentence in the dream held a significant message. While the daughter was seventeen and experiencing this traumatic event, the dreamer lost her serenity. This loss came while she was enjoying the actions and ideas of marriage and family life that she had so lovingly embraced. She was surprised to currently find herself in a position of enjoyment, where she was ready to give birth to a new productive life, but felt a strong sense that in order to do so she needed help.

After relating this dream, the dreamer mentioned that it was a powerful "feeling" dream and that being pregnant represented a new birth within herself, a new birth with a divine message. The dream manifested while attending a workshop that focused on internal healing. She went to the workshop expecting to achieve a new and healthier life with "hopes of getting better." This new life was verified in the dream by the symbolic forthcoming birth of her child. The dream presented an awareness of why she lost her serenity so long ago and has helped her to continue on a path of productivity creating a new and better life. She has begun to experience the comfortable feelings of serenity that were lost those many years ago.

Extra Sensory Projections

After recording a dream write down the events of the previous days, events that may have prompted the dream to occur. It is often assumed that daily events have no meaning and are just a reflection of daily experiences, when just the opposite is true. As was evidenced in the previous dream, an incident, event or emotion can form a part of the dream drama. This proves that it is often significant and relevant. The dream is usually given as an effort to solve a problem, receive divine guidance, represent a specific problem by bringing it to the attention of the dreamer or the dream could just be a reflection of the senses mingling with stored memories.

It is important to remember that physical senses continue being an influence while sleeping. They take an active part in our dreams. When the eyes are closed they still distinguish light from dark, including different forms of light. The light of an alarm clock could quite possibly inspire a dream about a fire, or the light of the moon may stimulate dreams of magical creatures. Auditory sensations also play a role in dream projections, for the body continues to hear external sounds when sleeping. It may be difficult to isolate specific sounds while awake such as dogs barking down the street or music drumming off in the distance, but sounds become clearly distinguished in sleep. These sounds can be somewhat altered and received through dreams as cars honking, people singing or other similar manifestations. Then there is the sensation of touch. When touch sensations join with other images, dreams of unusual and strange happenings can often occur.

A man once had a dream that someone was chopping at his arm with an ax. Upon awakening he immediately looked down to discover that he had a violent twitch in the muscle on his forearm. He mentioned that the dream seemed so real that he actually felt the chopping of the ax and thought for sure that when he woke up there would be a wound, but in reality, and to his relief, it was only a twitch in his arm.

A particularly profound, and somewhat private dream, was told to me by a woman who was experiencing massive hemorrhoid pain. Because of the physical pain and discomfort caused by the hemorrhoids, the woman's dress style, sitting, walking and sex life were altered. Then, one particularly troublesome night of pain and discomfort, she dreamed that she had a penis. She mentioned that it was rather large and in an aroused state throughout the entire dream. She couldn't fit comfortably in any of her clothing. It was so irritating and bothersome that she was filled with anger towards its presence! While in this state of irritation she also experienced feelings of extreme sexual arousal and couldn't seem to get enough attention from her husband. In a dream conversation she made the following comment to her husband, "Is this how you feel all the time?" Then she felt compassion toward him and apologized for feeling so insensitive concerning his needs. When she woke she realized that the physical sensations of the penis in the dream, with its discomforts and life altering influences, were similar to the physical experiences of hemorrhoids during her waking moments which literally affected everything in her life.

A young mother who loved watching a popular TV show about zombies had a disturbing dream one night. She was obsessed with watching a particular zombie show and viewed several episodes over a few days. During the mass viewing of the zombie show she experienced a dream where she became a zombie, devouring human flesh. She woke herself up with a deep guttural growl, bringing disgust to herself and her husband. The dream caused such a repulsive and negative emotion within the young mother that she decided to stop viewing the show with such vigor!

Another dream influenced by the senses occurred to a young man who had recently watched a movie about aliens. In the dream the young man found himself crawling on his belly toward a specific destination when the path he was on collapsed. He quickly discovered that he had fallen into a mushy type substance that revealed an alien buried to its torso. The young man tried to go the opposite direction, but got stuck in the muck! This dream, even though it was brought on by a sensory impression from a movie, also had symbolic meaning to the dreamer. During the time of the dream, the young man was in the final week of a difficult class in college. He was struggling to finish an important essay and was stuck on a specific detail. The manifestations in his dream of being "stuck in the muck," were in reality mirrored feelings of being "stuck in the muck" with regards to the writing of the essay paper.

General Outline for Recording Dreams

The following are a couple suggestions on ways to record dreams:

1. Use a phone recorder, or some type of electronic recording device. I use my phone which has access to a downloaded recording device. In the beginning of the recording, state your name and the date. After recording the dream, mention events happening in life at the time of the dream. Then record your first impression of the dream message. When finished, give the dream a title. Later, when you are awake and not rushed, while listening to the recording, type or write out the dream, insert the symbols and read the dream. The act of reading the dream often reveals a more detailed interpretation.

2. Use an outline and write the dream in a journal:

    Date

    Current events in your life

    Dream Setting: (Time and place)

    The Dream

    Final Sentences

    Feeling residue

Sensory Projections (If any can be recalled)

Interpretation

Outcome: (Action that may result from the educational experience of the dream)

Some people believe that the main purpose for sleeping and dreaming is to enable the mind to break identification with the habitual sense of self. Pictures are formed in the mind concerning personal perception. These pictures are composed of traits which are admirable, along with some traits that are not so pleasing. Since the moments of life are tied to self images, there may come a need to put aside these metaphors, which can be done through sleep. This sleep process can be liberating, releasing the mind from the perceived tensions and judgments regarding the dreamer's personal perception. A great deal can be done to relieve the pressures which have been placed upon the mind by learning to value the dream interpretation. Everyone can learn to use and direct their thoughts and emotions.

This book reveals methods of interpretation that can be used by anyone who dreams. The symbols, dreams and interpretations presented are illustrations of dream interpreting methods. They are examples of ways to arrive at ideas about the dream's meanings and how they can apply to a person's life. This book does not include information that requires intensive psychological training to understand. It is intended to assist the dreamer in becoming more aware of their projections and limit their judgments by becoming more objective in their beliefs.

Enjoy dreaming and interpret dreams when possible.

Showing a continued interest in dreams will help with learning more about them and their meanings. Scientists may never learn if butterflies dream, but like the butterfly, the dream is a cocoon that can provide security while learning to grow. This security can be a strength and inspiration as the soul language reveals an awareness of life's purpose. Dreams can be a revealing guide to help master emotions in the personal transformation into expanding brilliance!

"Sleep" by Walter De La Mare

Men all, and birds, and creeping beasts,
When the dark of night is deep,
From the moving wonder of their lives
commit themselves to sleep.

Without a thought, a fear, they shut
The narrow gates of sense;
Headless and quiet, in slumber turn
their strength to impotence.

The transient strangeness of the earth
Their spirits no more see;
Within a silent gloom withdrawn,
They slumber in secrecy.

Two worlds they have—a globe forgot
Wheeling from dark to light;
And all the enchanted realm of dream
That burgeons out of night.

Acknowledgements

It is with gratitude and pleasure that I acknowledge
the following people who have enriched my
life and helped to make this book possible:

My mother who is my hero

My husband who is my greatest support

My children who are some of my best teachers

My grandchildren for their enduring love and innocence

My family, friends and clients who willingly trust
me to guide them with their dream messages

My favorite authors who have inspired
me through the years

My editors Allen Smithson and Diane Hornaday
who devoted hours of work fine-tuning this book

My associations and promptings of the spirit, for
without spirit this book would not be created

Copyright Acknowledgments

For permission to use copyrighted material the author gratefully acknowledges the following:

"Marcian". *Catholic Encyclopedia*. New Advent. 2012. Web. 2014.

Bergson, Henri. *Dreams*. Trans. Edwin E. Slosson. New York: The Independent, 1913.Huebsch, 1914.

Clough, A.H. Ed. A.H. Clough. *Plutarch's Lives*. The Project Gutenberg: 1996. www.gutenberg.net. Ebrary. Web. 2014.

Cochran, Lin. *Edgar Cayce, On Secrets of the Universe and How to Use Them in Your Life*. Ed. Charles Thomas Cayce. New York: Warner, 1989.

Holy Bible: Authorized King James Version with Explanatory Notes and Cross References to the Standard Works of the Church of Jesus Christ of Latter-Day Saints. Salt Lake: Church of Jesus Christ of Latter-Day Saints, 1979.

McTaggart, Lynne. *The Intention Experiment*. New York: Simon & Schuster, 2007.

Pert, Candice B. *Molecules of Emotion. Why You Feel the Way You Feel*. New York: Scribner, 1997.

Raizizun, Yacki. *The Secret of Dreams*. The Project Gutenberg: 2004. www.gutenberg.net. ebrary. Web. 2014.

Smithson, Allen J. *The Parable of the Hand and the Glove, A Spiritual Awakening*. Bloomington: Abbott Press, 2012.

Tiller, William A., Walter E. Dibble Jr, and Michael J. Kohane. *Conscious Acts of Creation, The Emergence of a New Physics*. Walnut Creek: Pavior, 2001.

Truman, Karol Kuhn. *Feelings Buried Alive Never Die...* Las Vegas: Olympus, 1991.

About the Author

Laina was raised in Boise Idaho where she attended Boise State University majoring in Child Psychology. While attending Boise State, she entered the Miss Boise Pageant wining the talent award for singing a song from the famous opera "Marriage of Figaro" composed in 1786 by Wolfgang Amadeus Mozart.

While in her early twenties and before completing her college education, Laina began her homemaking career. She enjoyed birthing her children at home and being a home-schooling mom. She is the proud mother of four children and grandmother to eleven grandchildren.

As a Distinguished Toastmaster trained in leadership and public speaking and a Reiki Master Teacher, Laina is grateful for the opportunity to be a guide and bearer of light to others by sharing uplifting messages. For over sixteen years she has been an Independent Distributor with Young Living Essential Oils and has facilitated many classes and workshops about therapeutic essential oils, health and wellness, leadership and business building opportunities.

Laina enjoys spending time outside in her garden, taking long walks in the early morning, reading inspiring books and teaching private music lessons. Living near Sedona, Arizona with her husband is like living in a year round vacation spot. She loves being surrounded by the beautiful red rocks of Sedona while enjoying life with her friends and family.

To learn more about Laina visit her web site at
www.lainascorner.com